I BELIEVE

NEVIN C. HARNER

I Believe

A Christian Faith for Youth

The Christian Education Press
and United Church Press
1505 Race Street, Philadelphia, Pa. 19102

Printed in the United States of America

CONTENTS

INTRODUCTION

There is no unbelief,
Whoever plants a seed beneath the sod
And waits to see it push away the clod,
He trusts in God.

There is no unbelief,
Whoever sees, 'neath winter's field of snow,
The silent harvest of the future grow—
God's power must know.

There is no unbelief,
Whoever lies down on his couch to sleep,
Content to lock each sense in slumber deep,
Knows God will keep.

—LIZZIE YORK CASE

"I Believe" and "I Know"

"I BELIEVE" is different from "I know." Knowledge is one thing; belief, or faith, is another.

We know that two plus two equals four. We know that the sum of the angles of any triangle is a hundred and eighty degrees. We know that the distance around the earth at the equator is approximately twenty-five thousand miles. We know that the earth goes around the sun in three hundred and sixty-five and one-fourth days. We know that water is made up of two parts of hydrogen and one part of oxygen.

But when we come to our Christian faith, we find a somewhat different realm. Here we cannot move ahead quite so surely, nor prove things quite so neatly. Suppose, for example, that you were called before a judge and jury, and asked to prove to their satisfaction the truth of the following:

> That there is a God;
> That he is like Jesus;
> That he cares for us;
> That human history is in his keeping;
> That he hears us when we pray to him;
> That there is a life after death.

How would you go at it? What would you say? What evidence would you bring forward?

We Know Very Little

As a matter of fact, our knowledge is very slight, and the things we know are generally trivial and insignificant. On the contrary, most of the truly important matters, those by which and for which we live, can't be proved at all.

To begin close home, we can't prove that the sun will come up tomorrow morning. We believe that it will; it has always done so, and we assume that it will do so again; but we have no way of being sure. During a long cold winter, when the snow lies heavy upon the ground and all nature seems to be dead, we can't prove that spring will come again in due time. We can't prove that our parents love us, and will continue to do so. We can't prove that love is better than hate, or that forgiveness is better than revenge. In short, we can't prove anything that is truly important.

Not even the scientists can prove all they take for granted. A modern chemistry book is full of talk about electrons, atoms, and molecules. But up to this moment, no scientist has ever seen an electron in a microscope, or an atom; and only a few of the largest molecules have become visible under the most powerful microscopes. Does the scientist know with absolute certainty that electrons and atoms exist? No, he does not. Is the scientist wrong in assuming that electrons and atoms exist? No, probably not. Is his assumption pure guesswork? By no means. How then does he proceed? Well, the elements and compounds act as though electrons and atoms were present. There is good evidence pointing in that direction. So the scientist sets up what he calls an hypothesis, which is in full accord with what he does know, but goes considerably beyond it. Then he simply goes ahead and acts as though his hypothesis were true and could be proved in every particular. And things come out all right.

In other words, the scientist in his field—like all of us in daily life—walks by faith.

We Live by Faith

The truth of the matter is that we live by faith a great deal of the time. When we go to bed at night, we hang up our clothes, believing that the sun will rise on schedule time and that we shall get up and dress for another day. When the frost is still in the ground, the farmer gathers his seed together and prepares his machinery, believing that the spring will come and the earth will be ready for another crop. Young people in their teens lay their plans for college, believing that their parents are interested in them and will help to see them through. A young couple marry, believing in each other and in their capacity to face life and its difficulties together. A man places his hard-earned money in a bank, believing that it is well run, that its officials are honest, and that he can get his money back as he needs it. We climb aboard an overnight train and go peacefully to sleep, believing that the engineer is competent and sober, that everything along the right-of-way is in good order, and that we shall arrive safely at our destination.

All of this is faith, pure and simple. None of it can be proved. Yet we live by it every day and hour. If we were limited to things we can nail down with absolute proof, we could scarcely move about at all. In fact, the wisest course would be to make our way quietly to a dark room, and sit there the rest of our lives.

When we come to religious faith, the situation is precisely the same. As has already been suggested, most of the great Christian convictions can't be proved absolutely. They come under the heading of faith, not knowledge. They have to do with things unseen and eternal. As the Epistle to the Hebrews puts it: "Now faith is the assurance of things hoped for, the conviction of things not seen."

Does this mean that our Christian convictions are untrue? By no means! In this scientific age young people (and older ones too) sometimes get the notion that nothing is true unless you can find it in a test tube, or see it under a microscope, or work it out in an algebraic formula. What a terrible and tragic mistake! Your parents' love and concern for you can't be found in a test tube, nor seen under a microscope, nor worked out in an algebraic formula. Neither can the love of God! Nor the hope of immortality! Nor the matchless harmonies of a Chopin nocturne! Nor the far-off beauty of the Milky Way! Nor the goodness of Jesus! Nor the spiritual power of the Bible! Nor the abiding strength of the Church! Yet all of these are true in the deepest sense of the word. Only they belong to the realm of faith—not knowledge.

Does this mean that our Christian convictions are mere guesswork? By no means! They rest upon very good evidence; only they keep on going beyond the edge of the evidence in what is often and rightly called a "leap of faith." For example, the Bible tells us that no one has ever seen God; does it follow then that belief in God is mere guesswork? The exact opposite is the case! There are evidences all around us of God's existence. Indeed, it would be much harder to look at life and try to believe that there is no God than to believe in God with all our hearts. To be sure, we have to go beyond the evidence in our "leap of faith," but it is not a leap in the dark. Let us go back to the scientist once more. No scientist has ever seen an atom; does it follow that belief in the atom is mere guesswork? Not at all! There are many evidences of the existence of atoms, and the scientist makes his own leap of faith. So do we; and we are on just as sure ground as the scientist.

Does this mean that our Christian convictions are unreasonable? By no means! Here is another serious mistake that people have sometimes made, namely, to suppose that religious faith involves believing things that are unreasonable. Faith is just as reasonable as knowledge; the only difference is that it keeps on going after knowledge stops. The known facts may take us along a given road for, say, ten miles. Faith keeps on going ten or twenty or a thousand miles—in the same direction. It doesn't turn around and go against the facts. It simply goes on beyond the facts. It has to, for it is dealing with much bigger matters. Is your faith that your parents will stand by you four or five years from now unreasonable? Not at all! You couldn't prove it, if your life depended on it. But there is much evidence pointing in that direction. And so you make your leap of faith in the same direction as the facts, but beyond them. So is it with our faith in God, and Jesus, and all the other certainties on which we build our lives.

So don't worry too much if someone asks you to prove your Christian faith. Just admit freely that it can't be finally proved. It is faith, not knowledge. But it is not therefore untrue, or guesswork, or unreasonable. It is the greatest thing in the world. Thousands have held to it joyously, and lived by it triumphantly; and so can you.

What a splendid sight to watch a person going forward trustfully and bravely, walking by faith! How much better this is than holding back in fear, or becoming so hard-headed as to believe only what can be seen! The way to live is described by Studdert-Kennedy in his unforgettable poem:

> How do I know that God is good? I don't.
> I gamble like a man. I bet my life
> Upon one side in life's great war. I must,
> I can't stand out. I must take sides. The man
> Who is a neutral in this fight is not
> A man. He's bulk and body without breath,

Cold leg of lamb without mint sauce. A fool.
He makes me sick. Good Lord! Weak tea! Cold slops!
I want to live, live out, not wobble through
My life somehow, and then into the dark.

—G. A. STUDDERT-KENNEDY
From The Unutterable Beauty. *Used by
permission of Harper and Brothers.*

* * * * *

The Old Testament verses quoted in this book are from the King James
Version. The New Testament verses are from the Revised Standard Ver-
sion of the New Testament, copyrighted, 1946, by the International
Council of Religious Education, and are used by permission.

1

Sir, we wish to see Jesus.
—JOHN 12: 21

WE WOULD SEE JESUS

We would see Jesus; lo! His star is shining
Above the stable while the angels sing;
There in a manger on the hay reclining,
Haste, let us lay our gifts before the King.

We would see Jesus, Mary's Son most holy,
Light of the village life from day to day,
Shining revealed through every task most lowly,
The Christ of God, the Life, the Truth, the Way.

We would see Jesus on the mountain teaching,
With all the listening people gathered round,
While birds and flowers and sky above are preaching
The blessedness which simple trust has found.

We would see Jesus in His work of healing,
At eventide before the sun was set;
Divine and human, in His deep revealing
Of God and man in loving service met.

We would see Jesus; in the early morning
Still as of old He calleth, "Follow Me";
Let us arise, all meaner service scorning;
Lord, we are Thine, we give ourselves to Thee!

—J. EDGAR PARK
Copyright Congregational Sunday-
School and Publishing Society.

IN our endeavor to work out some of the details of our Christian faith, we begin with Jesus and we end with him. He is "the pioneer and perfecter of our faith." You may have noticed on the altar or communion table in your church two capital letters, the one an "A" and the other a strange symbol not found in our English language. These two are Alpha and Omega, the first and the last letters in the Greek alphabet. Their meaning, therefore, is clear; they say to us that Jesus is the "A" and the "Z" of our Christian faith. If we want to know what God is like, we turn to Jesus. If we want to know what we should be like, we turn to Jesus. If we want to know the meaning of life, we turn to Jesus. Our Christian faith centers in him.

Who Was He?

The known facts about his life can be quickly summarized. He was born at Bethlehem, a few miles south of Jerusalem, around 6 B.C. (The later scholars who redated history from his birth made a six-year mistake in their calculations.) He was reared in a devout Jewish home in the town of Nazareth in the northern province of Galilee. He had four brothers—James, Joseph, Simon, and Judas—and at least two sisters (Matthew 13:55-56). The father of the family followed the trade of a carpenter, and Jesus apparently learned this trade also. We have only one story from the whole of his boyhood and early manhood, the appealing account in Luke 2 of his visit to Jerusalem with his parents when he was twelve years old. The probability is that Joseph died sometime during Jesus' youth, because Joseph is never mentioned during the later years of Jesus' ministry. This would leave Jesus as the chief support of a large family, because he was the oldest son.

When he was about thirty-three years old, he laid down his carpenter's tools, and went south to the banks of the Jordan where his cousin John was preaching and baptizing. There followed a two-year ministry of preaching, teaching, and healing, in the course of which he gathered about him a band of twelve disciples and a few other followers, including several women. In or around the year 29 A.D. (these dates are somewhat uncertain, and it really doesn't matter) he was put to death by crucifixion, a form of execution which the Roman

14

government used with criminals. But his followers then and now have always believed that he is still alive.

That is about all we know concerning the facts of his life. They may be found in somewhat greater detail in four short books located at the beginning of the New Testament—Matthew, Mark, Luke, and John. You should read these books again and again for yourself. Any one of them can easily be read at a single sitting. Taken together, they are much shorter than the average Sunday newspaper. They are virtually the only source we have for the most important life ever lived on this planet. Now there are some six hundred million people in the world who bear his name, and all of western history has been redated from his birth.

What Was He Like?

This is an even more significant question. It doesn't make too much difference where he lived, or how long, or how he earned a living. But the sort of person he was makes all the difference in the world. For one thing, we who call ourselves Christians undertake to follow Jesus. What is the nature of this person we are following? In what direction does he lead us? And, for another thing, we Christians begin with Jesus when we try to think about God. We say that God is like Jesus, and Jesus shows us what God is like. It is all-important, therefore, to know what Jesus was like; because the end-result of our thinking about God depends so much upon this one starting-point.

1. *He was a real human being.* This may seem like a strange statement, and an unnecessary statement. You may say, Has anyone ever really doubted that Jesus was a human being? Yes, many have doubted it; and we are sometimes prone to forget it ourselves. The truth is that Jesus has meant so much to so many people, and has impressed them as being so God-like, that they have often glossed over his humanity. In fact, in the early Christian centuries there was a widespread opinion that Jesus had not really been born, and lived, and

suffered, and died. He had just *seemed* to be born, and live, and suffer, and die. And so it is necessary for us to remind ourselves that he was a real human being. He worked. He played. He laughed. He cried. He perspired with honest toil. He was tempted. He became discouraged. He suffered unspeakable pain on the cross, and revolted against it much as you and I would.

All of this brings him very close to us. He was not some ethereal creature, suspended halfway between earth and sky. Instead, he walked the earth as we do, and underwent life's joys and sorrows as we do. And all this brings God very close to us. If in some true sense the eternal God was in Jesus, walking up and down the hills of Galilee, then he is not a distant deity. He drew close to our flesh and blood that one time, and remains close always.

2. *He was a man, not a woman.* This may seem like another strange and unnecessary statement. Again you may say, Has anyone ever really doubted that Jesus was a man? In the strict sense of the term, No. But time and again men have made him effeminate in their mind's eye and in the portraits they have painted of him. During the Middle Ages painters were so anxious to catch the tenderness and gentleness of Jesus that they sometimes used women models. Tenderness and gentleness he had in full measure; he would not hurt a single soul. But he also possessed genuine manliness and masculine strength.

Think for a moment of what we know concerning his life. Take the simple fact that he must have supported a family of at least eight members by working day after day at the carpenter's bench. After some years of such a life, would he have lily-white hands, neatly and gracefully folded as some artists have depicted him? Hardly! Rather his hands would be strong and calloused; and his arms and shoulders heavily muscled.

Or take another known fact, namely, that rough and ready fishermen like Peter, James, and John left their nets and followed him. By no stretch of the imagination could they be regarded as sissies. They were outdoors men, making their living the hard way. They were hot-tempered men. Peter once snatched a sword and cut off a man's ear. And James and John were known as the "Sons of Thunder." Do you think they would have given their willing allegiance to someone who was effeminate?

It seems, therefore, that we must picture our Lord as having been strong and manly, for all his gentleness and tenderness. He was capable of attracting men as well as women into discipleship; and he still is. The Church is for men, as much as it is for women. Christianity is a man's religion as truly as it is a woman's religion. It has an appeal to all, and can meet the deepest needs of all, men and women, youth and children.

3. *He was very brave.* The best proof of this is the way he steadfastly set his face to go toward Jerusalem, even though he knew the capital city was the stronghold of his enemies. When he was in the vicinity of the Sea of Galilee, he might so easily have slipped off to the north toward Tyre and Sidon. Then he would have run into no danger. He would not have been crucified. And the chances are we would never have heard of him. Instead he did just the opposite. He knew that mortal danger lay ahead of him. But he was utterly devoted to the doing of God's will, and he was very brave. So he walked with steady pace into a hornet's nest of opposition.

By way of contrast, consider the founder of another religion, a man named Lao-tse who lived in ancient China. When circumstances became difficult for him, he simply drove out of the city gate, and was never seen again. As one memorable phrase puts it, he "withdrew into convenient irresponsibility." That is a good way to avoid the worries of life, and to live a long time. But it is a far cry from our Lord, moving step by step toward Jerusalem, where arrest, trial, torture, and death lay in wait for him.

There is a painting of Jesus standing in the judgment hall before Pilate. Not too far from him is a pillar, supporting the roof of the building. Jesus' body is parallel with the pillar, as straight and strong as it is, even though he knows full well that the man sitting before him has the power to condemn him to a cruel death. When you think of Jesus, think of that picture, and of his quiet, unresisting, unfearing courage straight to the end.

4. *He was in love with people, all kinds of people.* "In love" probably says it as well as anything else, although the words have a different meaning in Jesus' case from their usual significance today. He was not romantic, sentimental, or soft-hearted towards people. Rather, he liked people. He loved people. He cared for people. He wanted the best for people. He was willing to do anything for people. In fact, his whole mission and ministry were directed toward people. As he himself said: "I came that they may have life, and have it abundantly" (John 10:10). It was for people that he lived, taught, preached, healed, and finally died.

He loved all kinds of people. Rich people, like the rich young ruler; and poor people, like the widow who dropped a tiny coin into the collection box. Well educated people, like Nicodemus; and people with little formal education, like James and John. Good people, like Mary and Martha; and bad people, like Mary Magdalene. Well people, like the hale and hearty Peter; and sick people, the blind and crippled and diseased who came to him for healing. Sane people, and insane people. Old people, and young people. People one by one, and people in crowds and entire communities. Lovely people, and unlovely people. Jesus loved them all. Even his enemies came within the circle of his concern, and in the midst of his awful agony on the cross he prayed the Father to forgive them, because they really didn't know what they were doing.

Jesus' devotion to people knew no bounds or limits. It went all the way. It counted no cost. It stopped at no sacrifice. As one of his followers described it, "having loved his own who were in the world, he loved them to the end" (John 13:1).

18

Or, to use his own memorable words: "Greater love has no man than this, that a man lay down his life for his friends" (John 15:13). Beyond that, there is nothing more. Our Lord would be much easier to follow, if he had only loved others a little less.

5. *He was very close to God.* All his life he was close to God. God was more real and near to him than his mother Mary, or his brothers and sisters, or the carpenter shop where he worked, or the hill above Nazareth where he sometimes wandered to watch the setting sun. God was more real to him than anything else. And Jesus was more like God than any other person who ever walked this earth.

This closeness to God began quite early in his life. We don't know just when it started, but we do know that when he was only twelve he said, much to the amazement of those who heard him, "Did you not know that I must be in my Father's house?" (Luke 2:49). These, by the way, are the first words ever spoken by him, of which we have any record. Strange words they are! Most twelve-year-old boys don't speak in this fashion. Some twenty years later, when he had just started his public ministry, he said, "My food is to do the will of him who sent me, and to accomplish his work" (John 4:34). About two years later still, out of the torture of crucifixion he forced from his parched lips the words of quiet triumph, "It is finished." From start to finish, God, the love of God, and the will of God were the chief facts in his life.

It is little wonder that as the days went by the conviction dawned and grew upon those early disciples that in seeing Jesus they were seeing more than a man; they were glimpsing God himself. We can only imagine how they must have felt as this realization came to them, and became steadily stronger. How their eyes must have stared at him, as they saw him in this new light! How their minds must have stretched to take in the wonderful thought! How awestruck they must have been as they heard and wrote down his breath-taking words, "I and the Father are one" (John 10:30). Here in this carpenter's son from Nazareth was the mighty God, walking up and down the dusty roads of Palestine by their side! This was what God was like—loving, tender, strong, merciful, caring for people, suffering and dying with them!

Sooner or later they had to find words to catch up this world-changing experience. And they found them. They called him "Emmanuel," which means "God with us." That said it, in part at least. Then they went further still. They called him the "Son of God." The impulsive Peter must have fairly gasped the words, when he first ventured to say, "You are the Christ, the Son of the living God" (Matthew 16:16). Whatever else the words meant to Peter, or to the millions who have repeated them since that day, they surely carried the conviction that Jesus was as much like God in spirit and in nature as a son can possibly be like his father; that, as one of our modern scholars has put it, as much of God was in Jesus as can possibly ever be in a human being.

This is by all odds the most important item in our faith concerning Jesus. If people had not found God in him, and continued to find God through him, he would probably have been forgotten long ago. He would be just another prophet, another teacher, another good man; and the world has known many of these. But Christian faith has seen more in him. It has been unable to imagine anyone better, more noble, or more Godlike than Jesus. And so it has dared to say: "For God so loved the world that he gave his only Son, that whoever believes in him should not perish but have eternal life" (John 3:16). This is the very heart of our faith, at its highest and best.

Some Difficult Problems

You may have noticed that we have passed by thus far all mention of the virgin birth, the miracles of Jesus, and his physical resurrection. Good Christians differ sincerely concerning these matters, and it is not easy to discuss them briefly and helpfully. However, we must try.

Two of the four Gospels, Matthew and Luke, affirm that Jesus had no earthly father, but that God was his only father. Most Christians from the first century to our own day have believed this teaching, and it found its way a long time ago into the Apostles' Creed in the familiar phrase, "born of the Virgin Mary." It has been and is a very precious doctrine to millions of good people. It links Jesus with God unmistakably, and sets him apart in a quite different class from other men. On the other hand, some Christians find it hard to believe that Jesus had no earthly father. They say that God seems to have worked out a definite plan by which babies are born into this world, and it is likely that he would follow this same plan in Jesus' case. They point out also that Mark and John say nothing about the virgin birth; nor does any other book in the New Testament except Matthew and Luke. Besides, they call attention to the fact that it was common in our Lord's day to explain a great person by affirming that God (or one of the gods) was his father.

Perhaps the important thing here, as in so many like cases, is to go down to a deeper level, and locate a conviction that both groups can cling to. In this case it is the firm belief that in some manner and in some true sense Jesus came from God. That is what really matters. Is Jesus merely a product of hydrogen, oxygen, and carbon, and unable therefore to show us what lies at the heart of our perplexing universe? Or did his spirit come from God, and does he show us truly what God is like? The virgin birth is one way of holding to this basic conviction. It does so by making God the literal biological father of Jesus. But this is not the only way of holding to this same conviction. It is reasonable to think that Jesus grew in Godlikeness. Born into a pious home, in the midst of a God-revering people, schooled in the Old Testament, seeing God everywhere in the lilies of the field and the blind beggar by the roadside, turning often to him in prayer, living in constant fellowship with him—Jesus might conceivably have become steadily more Godlike until he and God were one in

21

spirit. The Bible itself testifies that he "increased in wisdom and in stature, and in favor with God and man" (Luke 2:52). God often uses the ordinary ways of life to accomplish extraordinary purposes.

If, therefore, you can believe in the virgin birth, well and good. You have a firm basis for your conviction that Jesus came from God. If you cannot believe it, do not worry about it, but in your own way hold fast to this same conviction. In either case, try to view with understanding those who differ from you.

As for the miracles, there can be no reasonable doubt that people found healing through their contacts with Jesus—the lame, the blind, the mentally ill, and many others. The miracle accounts are too numerous and too closely interwoven into all the Gospels to lead to any other conclusion. As a matter of fact, it would have been strange indeed if a person of Jesus' radiant faith in God and infinite compassion for people had moved about in a world full of physical and mental diseases without leaving people better than he found them. Whether these cures were brought about by a supernatural power above and beyond the laws which God has laid down for our healing, or whether they were done within the operation of these laws, is another matter. On this good Christians may disagree somewhat.

Harder to understand are the so-called nature miracles, such as the multiplication of the loaves and fishes, and the stilling of the storm on the Sea of Galilee. Again most Christians have believed these accounts to be literally true. But some have difficulty with them. They do not see anything of the sort happening today; they have learned in science courses that life seems to be governed by absolute and unchanging law; and they remember that everything now in the Gospels was handed down by word of mouth for a period of some years before it was committed to writing.

Again, if you can believe the miracle accounts in their literal form, well and good. Your appreciation of Jesus may thus be all the greater. But, if you cannot, do not reproach yourself. After all, the important thing about Jesus is who he was, what he was like, and what he means—not the marvelous acts reported of him. He himself did not want to be known primarily as a wonder-worker.

As for the physical resurrection of Jesus, all four of the Gospels tell of an open tomb and a risen body. However, the oldest account of all is in I Corinthians 15, and this does not mention either an open tomb or a risen body. Of one thing we can be absolutely sure: the early disciples were convinced beyond any shadow of a doubt that Jesus was not dead but was alive. That they were so convinced is the surest fact in human history. How else can we explain the transformation almost overnight of Peter, James, John, and the rest from a band of scared disciples into a company of fearless apostles? Something happened to bring about this change. Whether it was the sight of an empty tomb and a risen body, or an overpowering experience of their living Lord such as came to Paul on the road to Damascus, or something else less spectacular but just as convincing, does not matter primarily. What does matter is the sure belief, theirs and ours, that Jesus is not dead and gone, but is still alive today.

What Is He to Us?

Now we come to the crux of the matter. This Jesus, who lived and walked the earth so many years ago, and is alive forevermore in the presence of his Father and in the hearts of his faithful followers—what is he to us? Something? Nothing? Much? Little? Would your life be at all poorer, if you had never heard of him? Is it worth your while to try to know him better than you now do? Perhaps two words will gather up most of what he can mean, and should mean to each of us.

1. *He is Lord.* This means exactly what it says. He is our Lord and Master. We are to follow him, obey him, give ourselves to him, try to be like him. We are to seek the things he sought, love people as he loved them, and do God's will as he

did it. We shall never succeed perfectly, but we are to keep on trying. During World War II we read of fair-haired German youth going into battle and the hazards of sudden death with the cry, "Heil, Hitler," on their lips. They had given themselves to Hitler with utter abandon. What he said, they did. Where he led, they followed. With a like loyalty—but in a different spirit, and for an entirely different purpose—we are to devote ourselves with all we have and are to Jesus and his cause.

But the word "Lord" signifies more than this. The Greek word in the New Testament which is translated "Lord" was the title given in that old Mediterranean world to a god. So when the early disciples recited their simplest creed, "Jesus is Lord," they meant to say that he was divine. And we can and should mean the same thing. In some true sense, God was in Jesus. When he spoke, God was speaking. When he acted, God was acting. His spirit was God's spirit. And, therefore, when we follow Jesus, we are not following a mere man. We are also falling in step with the will of God. That is why he deserves to be followed so implicitly by each one of us. He is our divine Master.

2. *He is Savior.* This is the meaning of his name, "Jesus." "And you shall call his name Jesus, for he will save his people from their sins" (Matthew 1:21). Many, many people have had the experience of being saved from their sins into a richer, fuller, better life through Jesus. But it is not easy to put into words exactly how this happens. Perhaps it will help if we point out two specific ways in which he is our Savior.

In the first place, he saves us by showing us the way. When we are motoring through strange territory, a competent guide at a cross-roads can save us much time, worry, and perhaps disappointment—indeed he can keep us from getting lost—simply by pointing out the way. Jesus does this for us. Life itself is a pretty strange territory. There are many roads, some of which go downhill to defeat and destruction, and others of which take us upward and onward to eternal usefulness and happiness. Jesus is a good guide. He knows the way. He tells us about it. But—more than that—he *is* the way. He has walked it. He has lived it. If we go with him, we shall not get lost, but shall arrive safely at our destination.

But this is not all. When we have got on the wrong road (and all of us do at times), Jesus gently draws us back to God and to his will. He does this by showing us—not merely telling us, but actually showing us—what the love of God for us is like.

Dr. Walter Marshall Horton has a splendid illustration in his book, *Realistic Theology*, which helps to make plain this way in which Jesus saves us. It concerns a Christian Japanese, who became headmaster of a school in China at a time when Japan had invaded China. The headmaster's intentions were of the best. He truly cared for the boys in the school. He wanted to help them, and to live his own life into their lives. But he could get nowhere, for the boys did not understand him and did not trust him. Now there was one boy in the school who was so close to the headmaster that he understood and trusted him fully. And because of this one boy, the way was open for the headmaster to reach all his boys with his concern, and help them, and draw them into the right way. This, of course, is a parable. The headmaster represents God. The boys in the school represent all of us. And the one boy who was close to the headmaster represents Jesus. God cares for us unceasingly, and wishes the best for us. But we go on our own way, and do not always understand him. Then the love of God is blocked and thwarted. But Jesus clears up our misunderstanding, and through him God gets a chance at us. This is one way, probably the chief way, in which Jesus becomes our Savior.

This example may help us to understand what is meant by the word "atonement." It literally means "at-one-ment." When we drift away from God and his will, and a great and ugly gulf yawns between us and our Father, Jesus steps in to reveal God's true nature to us and the true picture of what we are doing or failing to do, and draws us back to God's side. Thus the gulf is closed; and what had been two, becomes one again. Only the example breaks down at one point: the boy in the story made no sacrifice, while Jesus paid a heavy price to draw men back to God.

There is a verse in the Bible over which we sometimes stumble. We wonder if perhaps it does not claim a little too much. It is The Acts 4:12: "And there is salvation in no one else, for there is no other name under heaven given among men by which we must be saved." But if there is anything to what we have been saying this verse may be right after all. Could it be true that in this atomic age when peril hovers over us constantly there is no other way in which our world and we ourselves can be saved except by following Jesus and yielding ourselves to God's love as we see it in him?

2

Show us the Father, and we shall be satisfied.
—JOHN 14: 8

SHOW US THE FATHER

The word God is only a picture-frame; all its value depends on the quality of portrait which the frame encloses. Into that old frame Jesus put a new picture so beautiful because of his own life, so inspiring and winsome because of his sacrificial death, that men never had so thought of God before and never since have been so moved, melted and transformed by any other thought of him. That is an amazing thing to have done. In this world where so many have groped after God, guessed about God, philosophized concerning God, the Master has lived a life of such self-authenticating spiritual grandeur that increasing millions of men when they wish to think about God can think nothing so true, so satisfactory, so adequate, as that the God they worship is like Christ. Even Paul, who had been brought up in the Old Testament's noblest ideas of God, gained a new name for him when he had met the Master: "The God and Father of the Lord Jesus."

—HARRY EMERSON FOSDICK
From The Modern Use of the Bible. *Published by The Macmillan Company. Used by permission.*

THERE is an old story of a little girl who was busily engaged with a pencil and a piece of paper. Her mother looked over her shoulder and said, "What are you drawing?" "I'm drawing a picture of God," was the reply. "But," the mother said, "nobody knows what God looks like." "They will, when I get through," said the little girl.

We may smile at this child's cocksureness on such a weighty matter, but deep in our hearts we wish we could be as sure as she seemed to be. For we can't help wondering what God is like. What is there, if anything, behind the things which we can see and hear and touch? Is there a Power, which has created the world and now keeps it going? Is there a Person, who knows about us and cares for us? Of all the questions that can be asked, these stand at the head of the list in importance.

What and Where Is God?

How simple it would all be if we could see God—just once! It may even seem a bit unfair of God to keep himself hidden and never allow us a single glimpse of him, forcing us to grope our way as best we can toward an understanding of him.

But wait a moment! Have you ever seen your mother? You have seen her body, in which she dwells and through which she shows her true self. As you read these lines, you have a clear mental image of her face and hands. But those are only flesh, bones, muscles, and nerves; they are not your mother. The truth of the matter is that you have never seen and will never see your mother—her spirit, her regard for you, her thoughts, her purposes. You are familiar with her body, within which she lives and through which she expresses herself, but not her inner self.

Perhaps we have in this illustration as good a way as any of understanding what and where God is. Perhaps the world about us—sun, moon, and stars; rocks, hills, and seas; electricity and light; even mankind and human history—may be thought of as God's body. This is where he dwells, and through all of this he expresses himself.

According to such a conception, God lives throughout his created universe. He is the chemical elements which make up the world about us. He is in the new life of springtime, and his is the power which makes the plants grow and the trees burst forth in leaf and flower. He is in the beauty of a sunset, and it is his beauty which is shining through. He is in human hearts and human history. He is present through it all, just as you—the real "you"—are to be found in head, arm, and toe. Prick any of these with a pin, and "you" feel it. "You" are there. If it seems difficult at first to picture God as being present in a rock or a tree, is it after all any harder than to picture "you" as being present in skin or fingernail? God's body is just a different kind of body—that's all!

To go a step further in our thinking, "you" are present throughout the strange mechanism which you call your body, but "you" are more than this body. You come to a focus somewhere (the best we can do is to picture this as happening in the brain). You know that you are you. You can look down on your body, as it were. You can make it do your will. You can say to it, "Walk over to the other side of the room," and it proceeds to obey. Perhaps in somewhat the same way God, while being ever-present in his body, comes to a focus somewhere and somehow. He knows that he is God. He can look down on his body ("down" may not be the right word, but let it stand). He can make it do his will. He is more than his body, different from his body, although present in it.

In this way of thinking, God does not have a body like ours. We would not picture him at all with a face and hands and feet, perhaps sitting on a golden throne. He has a body, but it is quite different from ours. Why should we imagine that ours is the only kind of body in the universe?

In this way of thinking, God is not up in heaven. Or, more accurately, he is in the heavens, and also here on earth. He is all around us and within us. He is "closer than breathing, nearer than hands and feet." There is no such thing as talking about God behind his back, or getting far away from him.

Notice finally that, in this way of thinking, we should not complain any longer over the fact that we are unable to see God. As a matter of fact, we can see him in just the same way that we see any other person. We see his body. We see what he does. We see the instrument through which he expresses himself. And that is all we can ever see of one another. God is a spirit, and spirits are invisible. Spirits are never in direct touch with one another (unless mental telepathy is now proved, as many think it is). But ordinarily between your spirit and mine stand two bodies—yours and mine. So is it with you and God. Between you and God stand two bodies—yours and his. But you are in just as close touch with him as you are with me, or with your mother.

What Is He Like?

Just as was the case with Jesus, the most important question concerning God is not where he is, nor what he looks like, but what he *is like*. In other words, what is his nature? What sort of being is he? The following statements regarding God represent the beliefs most commonly held by Christians:

1. *God is a Person.* That is to say, God is not a mere Law or a set of laws, somewhat like the law of gravity. The laws of nature and of human nature may be a part of him, or one of the ways in which he expresses himself; but God is more than that. Nor is God a mere Power or a set of powers, somewhat like electricity. The power that holds the stars in their places, or makes a rosebush grow, may be a part of him, or one of the ways in which he expresses himself; but God is more than that. God is a Person, as you and I are persons, only he is infinitely greater than we are.

What does this mean? It means that God is all that we are, and can do all that we can do, and much more besides. He is self-conscious. He knows that he is. He knows that he is God. He can think. He can feel. He can purpose, and carry out his purposes. Otherwise we would be putting God lower in the scale of being than we are, and that hardly seems reasonable. God may be more-than-personal, but he is scarcely less-than-personal.

What we believe about God in this regard makes a difference. You can work with a Law or a Power, and to a degree trust it; but you can't pray to it, or believe that it cares for you. This would be a rather lonely and friendless universe, if we could not believe that God is a Person.

2. *God is almighty*. He is all-powerful. By his hand (this is figurative language; for he does not really have a hand with five fingers) the heavens and earth were created. And he is still at work, still creatively active. He is in the growth of a grain of wheat into a plant. He is in the growth of a child into a man. He is in the slow development of larger and larger social groupings—first the clan, then the community, then the nation, and finally "one world." Like our forefathers of old, we stand in awe before the endless and ceaseless power of the Almighty, which our little minds can't begin to grasp.

But there are some things God can't do. There are limits to his power, limits which he has imposed on himself. It seems best to view the matter this way. There is no one or nothing outside God big enough to tell him what to do, or to interfere with his actions. But he can limit himself, and he seems to have done so. God, then, is self-limited.

He limited himself when he decided to set up an orderly and law-abiding world. Conceivably he could have made the world after an entirely different pattern. He might have created a universe in which water ran downhill in summer, and uphill in winter; or one in which two plus two made four on Monday, Wednesday, and Friday, whereas they totaled five on Tuesday, Thursday, and Saturday. But such a topsy-turvy creation apparently didn't look to be best for his purposes, or for his children. And so he made an orderly world, and, in so doing, limited himself. Now he can't make two plus two to equal five, nor gravity to pull uphill. He must be consistent with himself, the same from everlasting to everlasting.

God limited himself also when he decided to give men freedom of will to choose either good or evil. Conceivably he could have made us according to an entirely different pattern. He could have created us through thousands of years as mere blind machines, with no more freedom than an automobile engine. But that would not have done at all, because machines can't be children; and God seems to have wanted sons and daughters, whom he could love, and by whom he could be

31

loved in turn. So he took the awful risk of setting us free. As a result, he can't make us good against our will. He can show us the way, and make us restless until we find him and his will, and "spank" us back into line when we go wrong (as, for example, with a stomach-ache when we overeat), and suffer with us in our suffering, and draw us to him by the cords of his love. But we still have the God-given power to follow our own wills. We can be bad children. We can be mean, selfish, intemperate, stubborn. We can hold back, for a while at least, something that God wants very much (as, for example, a brotherly world in which all men and nations can dwell together in peace and happiness). How much God must have wanted children, to run risks like these!

3. *God is perfectly good.* He doesn't do anything bad. He doesn't think anything bad. He doesn't want anything bad. The thing that pleases him most is for us to be good, as he is good.

We Christians are so accustomed to this conception of God, that you may even think it strange to have the point mentioned. But people have not always pictured their deities as being good. Over in Japan the national faith, Shinto, has included a deity who on every count was a bad actor. His name is Susa-no-wo. On one occasion, according to Japanese legend, he wished to pester his sister, the sun-goddess. Among other mischievous pranks, he knocked down the divisions in her rice-fields, and carried filth into the room where she was celebrating a feast. How would you like to worship a god like that? How different is the picture in Matthew 5:48: "You, therefore, must be perfect, as your heavenly Father is perfect!"

4. *God is a Father.* We are now getting close to the heart of our Christian belief concerning God. God is not primarily a great Judge, or a great King. He is primarily a great Father. Try to picture all that a good father could possibly be; God is like that, only more so. He cares for us as an earthly father cares for his children, only more so. He wants the best for us —which may not always be what we think would be best for

us. He is lonesome, incomplete, and unhappy without us. He rejoices with us in our joy, and suffers with us in our sin and sorrow. When he judges or rules, he does so in a fatherly way.

This is the most daring conception ever to enter the mind of man, namely, that the Creator of heaven and earth, whose will is at work afar off in the Milky Way as well as in our backyards and in our own hearts, is a Father.

5. *God is like Jesus.* We might well have begun our description of God's nature with this, but in a sense it is better to end with it. This says all we have been saying, and more besides. For all Christians the essence of our faith in God is to be found in Jesus' own words: "He who has seen me has seen the Father" (John 14:9). Try then to call to mind a picture of what Jesus was like, and say to yourself, "God is like that." Did Jesus love all kinds of people, whether they were lovely or not? So does God. Did Jesus love them to the end? So does God. Did Jesus give himself for them? So does God. Did Jesus identify himself with them in their sin and suffering? So does God. Was Jesus very kind? So is God. Was he good? So is God. What things did Jesus care for more than all else? Whatever they were, those same things God cares for eternally.

It is a priceless privilege to believe in a God like Jesus, a Christlike God. If that is the kind of Spirit behind and within everything that is, we need not worry. In fact, we can't worry, no matter what happens temporarily to us and to the world about us. We may fall ill; people close to us may die; the world may descend into the bloody depths of war; but everything is in good hands. God cannot save us from all pain and sorrow; but his care goes with us all the way, and will finally bring us out into peace and happiness. Nobody knew this better than St. Paul. Hear his triumphant words of faith: "For I am sure that neither death, nor life, nor angels, nor principalities, nor things present, nor things to come, nor powers, nor height, nor depth, nor anything else in all creation, will be able to separate us from the love of God in Christ Jesus our Lord" (Romans 8:38-39).

One thing more: If we believe in a God like Jesus, we can't long be bad, and stay happy about it. We simply can't! We are haunted by the notion of God worrying about us, suffering with us, caring for us even when we don't deserve it, and trying to win us back to him and his way. Sooner or later we give in, and turn back.

How Do We Know All This?

Probably the only honest answer is, "We don't." This is Christian faith, not knowledge. We can't prove these things in the same way that we can prove a theorem in geometry. Moreover, God is so very great, and we are so very small, that the best we can know and believe now is probably only a tiny fraction of what there is to know and believe about him. We are about in the position in which Captain John Smith would have found himself, if he had tried to describe the whole North American continent after going inland a few miles from Jamestown. Nevertheless, there is good ground for believing each of the foregoing statements about God.

Begin with the world about you. Does it look as though it just happened? Daylight and darkness, summer and winter following each other with unwavering regularity; exactly one atom of sodium combining with one atom of chlorine to form ordinary table salt (and who told them to do it just this way?); animals breathing out carbon dioxide into earth's atmosphere, and plants "breathing in" carbon dioxide, and thus maintaining a balance; a grain of wheat always growing up into a wheat-plant, and never by mistake sprouting into oats or barley; marvelous colors all around us, and, to match them, an even more marvelous instrument called the eye with a retina capable of discerning colors; two tiny cells uniting and growing to form a baby, and then a man, with the capacity to master electricity, or write Hamlet, or compose the Moonlight Sonata; mankind making its precarious way up from caves and trees to skyscrapers and airplanes—did all of this just happen? Or did Someone create it, and create it this way? If some day along the roadside you found a beautiful watch with its many intricate parts delicately fashioned and fitted together, would you conclude that the watch just happened? Or would you begin to look around for a watchmaker?

Go a step further! There seems to be Something back of the universe, but is it Someone? Is God a Person? Well, we are persons; and, if God is less than personal, then whatever created us succeeded in making something higher than it is. That doesn't seem to make sense. Or say the same thing another way. We persons appear to be the top level of a long evolutionary process. At least we can do some things that rocks, plants, and animals can't do. Through countless centuries of evolutionary development, we have come out of this universe. But, if personality was not already there at its center, then the universe produced something higher than itself. This is like saying that water unaided rose above its own level. All of this doesn't seem to make sense either. Any way you take it, God can't reasonably be pictured as lower in the scale of being than we are. Therefore, he must be at least a Person, however much more he may be.

Go a step further still! As we have said earlier, Christians picture God as being like Jesus. They begin with Jesus, and move Godward from him. This is a tremendous leap of faith, to affirm that the mighty God is like Jesus, or that Jesus reveals to us the nature of God (both statements mean approximately the same thing); but is it an unreasonable leap of faith? If God is not as good as Jesus, then once again the universe brought forth something higher than itself, and water rose above its own level. But such things just don't occur. So, after all, it is reasonable to move from Jesus to God in our thinking; to start with the highest we know, and move from that to the Unknown. How else would you go at it?

Our belief in a personal Christlike God is faith, not knowledge; but it is a reasonable faith. It goes beyond the known and proved facts, but it fits what we do know better than anything else we can imagine. Let us therefore hold and de-

35

clare it without apology, and with deep satisfaction. It is our most precious possession.

Father, Son, and Holy Spirit

Again we have put off to the last a teaching which is difficult to explain, but is well worth the effort. It is the teaching of the Trinity, three Persons and one God—Father, Son, and Holy Spirit. The word "trinity" is not found in the New Testament (it did not appear in Christian thought until about 200 A.D.), but the basic ideas are there. It represents an old, old belief, which has held a depth of meaning to Christians all through the years. But to some it has been a stumbling-block. Modern Unitarians take a stand against trinitarian belief, and call themselves Unitarians by way of contrast. And quite a few Christians do not know quite what to make of it.

What does it mean, this doctrine of three Persons and one God? Does it mean that we believe in three separate gods—Father, Son, and Holy Spirit? No, we can rule out such an interpretation without too much difficulty. It all seems to have begun in people's experience, as doctrines generally do. The early Christians had such a rich and full experience of God that no single statement would express it, and they had to say three things at once to get it all in. That was the beginning. As devout Jews, which most of them were to begin with, they had long known and believed in the God of the Old Testament, the Creator of all that is, the Father of all mankind. But this same God had within recent years drawn much closer to them in Jesus of Nazareth whom they looked upon as the Son of God. And after Jesus left this earthly scene, the same God was still in their midst as a comforting and abiding Presence, a Holy Spirit. Suppose now all this had happened to you; how would you have put your experience into words in order to make it plain to someone else? Maybe you would have said something like Ephesians 2:18: "For through him (Jesus) we . . . have access in one Spirit to the Father." Maybe you would have begun to talk about three Persons and one

God—Father, Son, and Holy Spirit—because only in that way could you have done justice to what you felt to be true.

But what about this word "Persons"? Doesn't that seem to suggest three different individuals, three separate gods? To get into the clear on this point, we must dig back into the history of this word a bit. The Latin "persona" comes from two words meaning "to sound through." Strange as it may seem, its first meaning was the mask which a player wore in the theatre; then it came to mean the player himself; later still it signified an individual, a separate and distinct "person," just as it does today. When the Christians who spoke Latin began searching for language to express what they believed about God, and hit upon this word "persona," it seems to have been somewhere between the second and the third of these stages; but they themselves did not fully agree with one another on its exact meaning. We shall not be far wrong if we say that when the followers of Jesus first talked of three Persons and one God they meant something like this: We believe in one God, who has showed himself to us in three different roles—Father, Son, and Holy Spirit; just as the same actor can play three different parts. They did not have in mind quite what we have when we use the word "Persons."

Christians have tried again and again to find illustrations which would make clear what they meant by the Trinity. Tertullian around 200 A.D. thought of it as being somewhat like three different officials carrying out three different tasks in one and the same government. Athanasius a hundred years later likened it to the fact that the same man can be at the same time a father, a son, and a brother. And Augustine, a hundred years later still, compared it to memory, understanding, and will, three different yet closely related functions within the same mind.

It is clear then—is it not?—that the doctrine of the Trinity was not intended to mean that the Father is one God, and Jesus is a second God, and the Holy Spirit (or Holy Ghost) is a third God. Rather it meant that the one God had showed himself to men in three different ways, and men on their part had experienced him in three different ways. That is what it still means. It is a set of words in which Christians have tried to catch up what is really too deep for words: the fullness of God's nature and of his gracious dealings with his children; and the richness of men's experience of God. If people long ago had not worked out some such statement as this, we would have to do it for ourselves today.

Do you believe in God the Father, who made the world and upholds and governs it by his fatherly hand? Do you believe that in Jesus God showed his face to men most clearly, and walked among them to draw them tenderly back to himself? Do you believe that God is still alive and active in the world about us, and in our hearts within us? If you believe these things, you believe in the Trinity.

3

What is man, that thou art mindful of him?
—PSALM 8:4

WHAT IS MAN?

Behold what wondrous grace
The Father hath bestowed
On sinners of a mortal race,
To call them sons of God.

—ISAAC WATTS
English hymn writer, 1674-1748

My will is not my own
Till Thou hast made it Thine;
If it would reach a monarch's throne
It must its crown resign;
It only stands unbent
Amid the clashing strife,
When on Thy bosom it has leant,
And found in Thee its life.

—GEORGE MATHESON
Scottish writer and philosopher,
1842-1906

HERE we are on a planet, spinning through space. From the level of our eyes a couple of yards above its surface, it looks flat and stationary; but we know that it is actually round and moving at incredible speed. In comparison with the spaces between the stars it is a speck of dust, the head of a pin. Around the white-hot interior of our earth is a thin paper-like crust of land and water, and encircling it in turn a tiny, precious layer of air to breathe. This is our home.

We have been here a good while. Perhaps half a million years ago man became man. Slowly and painfully we have climbed the slope of civilization. Tens of thousands of years went by, and our ancestors learned the secret of fire, and the principle of the wheel. Within the past century men have found out more about our earth-home than during all the preceding centuries put together. Now we are able to use the power of steam, electricity, and the atom.

There are more than two billion of us now. Most of us are about five or six feet tall when we are grown. We walk upright on two legs, using our other two "legs" to make a living in a variety of ways. We are brown, yellow, white, red, and black. We cover our bodies with cloth, fur, and leather. We talk to one another in hundreds of different languages. We travel about the surface of our earth a good deal, some in ox-carts, others in supersonic airplanes. We have a particular aptitude for killing one another, and every now and then go on a murderous spree which we call a World War. At the same time, we are rather fond of music and art, and generally kind to babies and elderly people.

Who are we? How shall we think of ourselves? What is man?

A Drugstore Answer

An answer frequently given is that a man is two or three dollars' worth (the sum goes up with higher prices) of iron, phosphorus, calcium, carbon, and the like. This is a drug-store answer; a chemical answer; a bitter answer. It leaves us with very little importance in the scheme of things.

If this is the right answer, it makes little difference what we do on a date. After all, a boy is only a couple of dollars' worth of chemicals, and a girl is the same (believe it or not). Let the chemicals interact pretty much as they please; it really doesn't matter.

If this is the right answer, it makes little difference whether we get drunk or not. If we are only an assortment of chemicals, the addition of a few more won't matter much one way or another.

If this is the right answer, there is no point in becoming hot and bothered about the wages and working conditions of laborers in industry. If each laborer is only a combination of chemicals, he might as well be thought of simply as a hired "hand," or "foot," or "back," or "brain." We might as well get out of him all we can, and not bother too much what happens to him meanwhile.

If this is the right answer, there is nothing seriously wrong about lining up thousands of young men periodically as cannon-fodder. Chemicals can be used in a variety of ways, and this may be as good a way as any. These organisms will die sooner or later anyhow, and return to the earth to enrich it. It might just as well be sooner as later.

If this is the right answer, it makes little difference how we treat people of other races. Chemicals don't have any particular rights. If they are herded in slums, or segregated from other chemicals of a different color, or strung up to die in a lynching party, what's the difference!

If this is the right answer, democracy is about as good as autocracy, and vice versa. Shortly before World War II, one of our missionaries was talking to a Japanese police captain in a second-floor room along a busy street. Down below an old peasant shuffled along in his straw shoes. The captain said: "Do you see that old fellow down there? We don't care *that* about him (snapping his fingers as he spoke). Bring a million like him together, and we do care. The group and the nation count; the individual not at all." Such a view is entirely in order, if this is the right answer.

But is this the right answer?

A Scientific Answer

When we turn to the sciences, biology, physiology, psychology, we get a more respectful estimate of man. They point out, first of all, the marvels of man's body. Consider, for example, the following:

A digestive apparatus takes in food of various kinds, grinds it to bits, adds the proper chemicals at successive stages, and transmutes it into energy.

A few pints of blood course endlessly through arteries and veins, carrying nourishment to every cell, and carrying off waste products.

The heart contracts and expands, contracts and expands, minute after minute, year after year—the most perfect engine the world has even seen.

A delicate "thermostat" holds the body temperature at approximately ninety-eight degrees in winter and in summer, indoors and outdoors, rarely fluctuating by a fraction of a degree.

A small gland at the base of the brain, called the pituitary, regulates the growth of the skeleton of the body. If it overacts, the result is a giant. If it underacts, the result is a dwarf. But in ninety-nine cases out of a hundred, it does things just right.

A sperm, which unites with an egg to form a new baby, weighs a billionth of a gram and there are 450 grams to a pound. Within the nucleus of the sperm are twenty-four strings of beads called chromosomes, the longest of which is one ten-thousandth of an inch long. Each of these strings contains several hundred or more genes, all in a fixed position. These genes determine the color of the eyes which the new baby will have, the color of his hair, the texture of his hair, the amount of his hair, the shape of his finger nails, and even how long he is likely to live.

At the back of the eyeball is a sensitive membrane called a retina, which picks up light-waves of different length and sends on messages to the brain which we identify as colors— red, yellow, blue, and all the rest.

In the ear is a shell-like arrangement which registers sound-waves of varying rates of vibration, passes on messages to the brain, and we hear C, E, and G as a chord and like the sound of it.

But this is not all science has to tell us about ourselves. Psychology steps in to add still further marvels, such as this one:

The human brain may be likened to the central switchboard of a telephone system, with innumerable wires running out in various directions. This switchboard contains millions upon millions of nerve cells. The number of interconnections among these cells has been estimated to be the figure "1" followed by fifteen million "o's." Just to print this figure would require thirty books of three hundred and fifty pages each. Nobody has a name for such a number. Nobody can even imagine what it means.

Something like the foregoing is science's answer to the question, What is man? If this is the right answer, we must change our policy at some of the points mentioned in the preceding section. For example, it seems like a shame to pour enough alcohol into the system to confuse and benumb such a wonderful mechanism. And it begins to look like an awful crime to send thousands of these marvelous brains, even though covered with metal helmets, into a battlefield, where nitroglycerine and steel will rip some of them to pieces.

But do we now have the full story of what man is?

A Christian Answer

The Christian way of looking at man finds little truth in the drugstore conception. It accepts everything that the scientists have to tell us about man, but goes further still to formulate its own answer. What is that answer?

1. *We are children of God.* The Christian faith at its highest and best dares to believe that God is our Father, and we are his children—every last one of us. This is a new way of viewing these strange two-legged creatures that inhabit this tiny planet. If we are God's children, we are somewhat like him; because children generally "resemble" their parents. We are made in God's image. We can to a degree think his thoughts after him. We can to a degree want the same things he wants. We can to a degree be like him in spirit, kind as he is kind, unselfish as he is unselfish. We can live forever, as he is eternal. And if we are God's children, we are infinitely

43

precious in his sight. No one of us is to be disregarded or treated disrespectfully.

This changes things considerably!

If this is the right answer, it makes a great deal of difference what a boy and a girl do on a date; because the boy is a child of God, and so is the girl. Neither one has any business acting otherwise than as a child of God; and neither one has any right to view the other in any fashion except as a child of God. Your first reaction may be that this is likely to cramp your style sharply. It doesn't eliminate having a good time, because God wants us to enjoy ourselves properly in his world. It doesn't eliminate falling in love, because God has made the sexes attractive to each other. But it does rule out acting as though you were nothing but a body, and it also rules out viewing the other person as nothing but a body. A good many young people have been sorry the next morning, when they have forgotten the night before that they were children of God.

If this is the right answer, it makes a great deal of difference whether we get drunk or not. Children of God have no business getting drunk. The image of God within them should not be effaced, even for a few hours, by chemicals. And if they do get drunk, they are likely to do some things which are not suitable for God's children.

If this is the right answer, there is much room for concern over the wages and working conditions of laborers in industry. For each laborer is no longer a "hand"; he is a child of God. So is the foreman. So is the manager of the plant. So is the owner. Each one deserves to be treated in a manner befitting what he really is.

If this is the right answer, we must bend every effort to wipe war off the face of the earth. Our own young men are children of God. They have no business being turned into cannon-fodder. And the people on the other side are children of God too, and must be treated as such. When a bomb falls on a city, either our own or the enemy's, and sends thousands of people

44

scurrying for bomb shelters, mangling those who do not make it, and destroying the homes built up so patiently and tended so carefully, that is a terrible denial of the teaching that we are all children of God. We must stop it—and soon!

If this is the right answer, it makes all the difference in the world how we treat people of other races. For, you see, in this way of looking at people, the color of skin, the shape of nose, and the texture of hair don't matter. What matters is that beneath these externals every last one is a child of God, and is precious in his sight.

If this is the right answer, we must strive for something like democracy. The name doesn't matter, but the form of government does. It must be such as will respect every single individual—the Japanese peasant shuffling along in his rice-straw shoes, the soft-handed nobleman, the coal-blackened miner, the stoop-shouldered share-cropper, the laborer in overalls, the mother at the kitchen sink, the children running home from school—and give each one a chance to become the best of which he is capable.

The Christian view of man contains dynamite for both our personal and our social life.

2. *We are sinners.* This is the other half of the picture. A child can't stop being a child, but he can be a bad child. He can turn against his father. He can set what he wants over against what his father wants. He can even leave his father's house, and strike out on his own. So is it with us and God. We can't escape being his children, but we can be bad children. We can turn against our Father. We can set what we want over against what he wants. We can even leave the Father's house, figuratively speaking, and strike out on our own as though we were self-sufficient. For God has made us free to choose our own ways, even to the point of turning against him. This was the chance he took, when he chose to have children instead of mere blind machines.

And we often *are* bad children, all of us. If we think that we are not, either we don't realize what we are actually like,

45

or else we don't have a clear picture of what we ought to be like. The hardest child to deal with is the one who is really a bad child, but thinks all the while he is just about perfect. Similarly, God must scarcely know what to do with us when, sinners that we are, we stand boldly before him with no sense of anything wrong in our lives.

We need to be very clear as to what sin is. The word itself has in common usage become pinned down to a few obvious misdeeds, some of them major and others quite trivial. In ordinary speech it may take in card-playing, dancing, attending a baseball game on Sunday, staying away from church, swearing, lying, stealing, drinking, sexual immorality, and murder. But sin is much deeper and broader than these. As a matter of fact, this list includes a few acts which may not be sinful at all; and it leaves out some of the worst sins of which we are capable.

In essence, sin is putting our wills over against God's will, and setting ourselves up as the last word in place of God. Perhaps the best way to express this is to say that sin is Jesus' prayer in the Garden of Gethsemane in reverse. Jesus said, "Not my will, but thine, be done" (Luke 22: 42). When our lips, our attitudes, our lives say, "Not thy will, but mine, be done," that is sin.

Sin, then, is first of all a matter between God and us, but it comes out in a variety of forms, many of which involve our relationship with other people. Sin is primarily an inner bent of our personalities, but it shows itself in the things we do. Here are some of the telltale evidences of inner sinfulness:

To be proud of what we have, or what we are, or what we can do; whereas everything we have, or are, or can do comes either from other people or from abilities with which we were endowed, and originates ultimately in God himself.

To be thoughtless or ungrateful regarding our many blessings; whereas God gives them all to us, not because we deserve it so much as simply because he loves us.

To think that we are pretty "hot stuff," and can go it alone;

46

whereas we wouldn't have lived to be a week old if someone hadn't taken constant care of us, and we would all be dead if the supply of oxygen in the atmosphere were cut off for five minutes.

To be continuously on the look-out for "Number One"; whereas God wants us to seek the well-being of all people, as he does.

To fritter half our time away on drugstore corners; whereas God is hoping we will make some good use of the talents he has given us.

To live for eating, drinking, and making merry; whereas God isn't so much interested in our bodies which die, as in our spirits which do not.

To misuse our bodies in overeating, drinking, lack of exercise, and the like; whereas God has given us these bodies as a trust to be used in his service.

To choose a vocation with an eye to hard cash alone; whereas a true vocation is a calling from God to serve him and his children and advance his kingdom.

To be mean, cranky, or ill-tempered; whereas God wishes us to be kind and patient, as he is kind and patient.

To roll a choice bit of gossip on our tongues and pass it along with a gleeful smile; whereas God doesn't have it in him to hurt anyone, and wants us to be like him.

To look down on another person because he belongs to another race or nationality or hasn't been to college, or eats peas with a knife, or can't afford a big convertible; whereas God views every person as one of his children.

To be warm all winter and full-of-stomach three times a day, and read of European and Asiatic children in heart-rending misery, and turn over to the comics with never a second thought; whereas God does not desire the least of these to perish, and must be grieving his heart out over their sufferings.

All of these are sure signs of sin. If you find them in yourself, you are a sinner. Aren't we all?

We human beings are strange creatures. We are a mixture of body and spirit. We are children of God, and we are sinners. We have it in us to rise very high, and to fall very low. We can give ourselves to beautiful music, art, and literature; and we can overeat as no self-respecting pig would ever do. A recent popular magazine carried a full-page picture of all the people, surgical instruments, and medicines required to save the life of a boy who had the skin burned off a large portion of his body. We are like that! But we also on occasion turn our best brains, our factories, our man-power to the task of killing as many of the "enemy" and wiping out as many of their cities in as short a time as possible, before they can do the same to us. We are like that too! One museum carries endless exhibits of the things we have invented and manufactured to save life and make it enjoyable. Another museum displays instruments of torture like the thumb-screw and the rack. We make good resolutions—and break them! We are a puzzle and a worry to ourselves, and don't know what to do about it. Perhaps we all know how St. Paul felt when he wrote: "For I do not do the good I want, but the evil I do not want is what I do. Wretched man that I am! Who will deliver me from this body of death" (Romans 7:19, 24)?

All of this comes out to a couple of conclusions. The one is that our need to be saved is something more than "filler" used by preachers to take up the time in a Sunday morning sermon. It is a very real need for us all. We shall have to wait until a later chapter for further discussion of this point. The other is that we are incomplete until we give ourselves to God. This we can take up now.

3. *We are not ourselves till we are God's.* The strangest fact about human nature is this: we are never fully happy, or free, or all that we could be, until we simply place ourselves in God's keeping and devote ourselves entirely to his will. We are so made that this is what we need. Until this happens, we fret. We worry. We run around in circles. We try, and get nowhere; and sometimes the harder we try, the less headway

we make. We can become what we want to be finally not by trying at all, but by giving in. This is difficult to understand, but we must make a valiant effort.

Perhaps we are somewhat like a railway locomotive. If it becomes headstrong and leaves the tracks to follow its own course, it gets nowhere. But if it takes to the tracks once more, the shiny rails which hedge it in and would seem to destroy its freedom actually enable it to get somewhere. In the same manner, so long as we are on the way which God has laid down, we make progress. Otherwise, we don't. This is part of the truth we are driving at, but not all of it.

Let us try again, drawing upon psychology. We can't fully succeed in being happy by trying to be happy; because the harder we try, the more painfully self-conscious we become, and the unhappier we are. Neither can we fully succeed in being good by trying to be good; because the harder we try, the more self-centered we become, and self-centeredness is not goodness. So the only way to be happy and good is to lose ourselves in something outside ourselves, some interesting and helpful cause or activity, and lo! one morning we wake up to find ourselves happier and better than we could have become by aiming straight in that direction. Now there is nothing higher or greater in which to lose oneself than God and his will. Therefore, if we give ourselves to him and his purposes without reserve, we find happiness, goodness, and fullness of life sneaking in the back door. This also is part of the truth we are driving at, but not all of it.

Let us try once more. If we are made in God's image, then he is now all that we ought to be, and can be, but are not yet. He is the goal of our beings. He is the direction in which we are meant to move. The closer, therefore, we move toward him, the more fully we become what we were destined to be. Strangely enough, the more we bend our wills to his, the stronger they grow. The more we submit ourselves to him, the more fully we become our true selves.

Fifteen hundred years ago Augustine said that God has

made us for himself, and our souls are restless until they rest in him. Close to our own time the blind poet, George Matheson, wrote the hymn,

> Make me a captive, Lord,
> And then I shall be free.

The last verse is found at the head of this chapter. It seems to be utter nonsense, but maybe it is the best sense in the world. Try it out, and see for yourself.

4

The word of our God shall stand forever.

THE WORD OF GOD

The time has come for us to take up again the Old Book. It may have something in it which we have lost sight of and which we cannot get on without. We have been ashamed of it because of its antiquated science; but possibly it is not science which we need. We need religion, a new vision of God, a new contact with God in Christ. The ancient wise man may be right after all—"The fear of the Lord is the beginning of wisdom." The Hebrew preacher may have made no mistake when he said, "Fear God and keep his commandments, for this is the whole duty of man." We have the higher education, but it is evidently not high enough to get us where we ought to be. We have the new chemistry and the new psychology, but they do not give us a new heaven or a new earth. The Divine Library may hold a secret without which we cannot prosper. It may be that we shall never get out of our distresses until with one accord we begin to search the Scriptures.

—CHARLES EDWARD JEFFERSON
From The Bible in Our Day. *Published by Oxford University Press, Inc. Used by permission.*

Take out your Bible, and look at it. It is a large book. A typical copy will contain almost a thousand double-column pages in small type. It is really a library of sixty-six separate books. Some of them are quite long, while others are as short as a single chapter. It is divided into two parts, the Old Testament and the New Testament. The former is approximately three times as long as the latter. If you flip it open about at the middle, you will come close to the Psalms;

and if you divide the second half in two, you will be near the beginning of the New Testament. The Old Testament was written before Jesus, and the New Testament was written after him. The Old Testament was first set down in Hebrew, and the New Testament in Greek. The whole Bible took about a thousand years to complete, six times the length of time our nation has been in existence. It contains almost every imaginable type of literature—history, stories, sermons, poetry, orations, letters, laws, and even riddles. In some cases we know who wrote a book, when it was written, where it was written, and to whom it was written. In other cases we cannot be sure at any of these points.

The Bible is not the only sacred book in existence, but to us it is unique. Christians have long regarded it as the Word of God. What does this mean? And what value can the Bible have for us?

How Does God Speak?

If God is a Father, he would want to speak to his children. It is a poor father who has nothing to say to his children, or is not on speaking terms with them. God would want to tell men what he is like, what life is about, and what they should be like. Suppose now that God has no body like ours with vocal cords, lips, and tongue. Then he would not speak in the strange sounds which we call language—Hebrew, Latin, German, English, and the like. Instead he would choose other ways. As a matter of fact, we ourselves use a good many different ways of communicating with one another. Sometimes a shrug of the shoulders, or a wave of the hand, or an expression of the face will speak volumes. On other occasions we talk to others simply through what we are. You have often heard the quotation, "What you are speaks so loudly, I cannot hear what you say." So our own speaking is not always limited to speech, in the usual sense of the word. But, to return to God, if he had something to say to his children, how would he go about it?

52

Well, to begin with, he would welcome gladly a sensitive people, who would be alert to what he had to say. Such a people he seems to have found in the Hebrews, an ancient nation living on a bridge of fertile land with the Mediterranean Sea to the west of them, and desert to the south and east of them. For some reason or other, the Hebrews were an unusually sensitive people in matters of religion. The Greeks had a genius for art, and the Romans had a genius for government, but the Hebrews had a genius for religion. They are often referred to as "the chosen people"; maybe that is saying the same thing in different words.

God did not speak to the Hebrews alone. As the Bible itself says: "He did not leave himself without witness, for he did good and gave you from heaven rains and fruitful seasons, satisfying your hearts with food and gladness." That sort of speaking he has done through all the years to all the peoples of the earth. But either he said more to the Hebrews than to the others, or else they understood him better.

First of all he spoke to them through the wonder, the order, the beauty, and the fruitfulness of nature. And they understood what he was saying. The Old Testament especially is full of what nature told them about God, his majesty, and his gracious provision for man's needs. To take a single example, Psalm 19 begins: "The heavens declare the glory of God; and the firmament showeth his handiwork. Day unto day uttereth speech, and night unto night showeth knowledge."

Then he spoke to them through history, particularly their own. The Hebrews have never had an easy time of it. Their homeland was exposed to attacks from all nations, and time and again the tread of foreign armies was heard on Hebrew soil. Through the ups and downs of their existence they gradually caught on to some eternal truths which God was revealing to them. They learned, for example, what is now recorded in Proverbs 14:34: "Righteousness exalteth a nation: but sin is a reproach to any people."

He spoke to them also through great and good men, who rose up among them and were unusually sensitive to what he had to say—Moses, Elijah, Isaiah, Jeremiah, Amos, Hosea, Micah, and many others. No other nation, large or small, has ever had an equal array of such men. We often speak of them as God-inspired, and so they were, in that they were quite close to God's Spirit and uniquely receptive to what he had to say to them. Take, for example, Isaiah, that brilliant young nobleman of the eighth century before Christ, who never till the closing years of his life got far away from the Temple in Jerusalem, and went about with his hand to his ear, as it were, to hear what God was saying. Having heard it, he passed it on to others, as in this striking passage: "Hear the word of the Lord, ye rulers of Sodom; give ear unto the law of our God, ye people of Gomorrah. To what purpose is the multitude of your sacrifices unto me? saith the Lord: I am full of the burnt offerings of rams, and the fat of fed beasts; and I delight not in the blood of bullocks, or of lambs, or of he goats. . . . Wash you, make you clean; put away the evil of your doings from before mine eyes; cease to do evil; learn to do well; seek judgment, relieve the oppressed, judge the fatherless, plead for the widow" (Isaiah 1:10-11, 16-17). That was fairly straight talk, but Isaiah had to say it, because he felt it came directly from the Lord. Who will venture to say he was wrong?

Then finally, when they were ready for it, he spoke to them and to all men through one God-filled life, that of Jesus of Nazareth. This was the clearest speaking God ever did. Here was God's word lived out so unmistakably that all could see it and understand. As the Gospel of John records it: "And the Word became flesh and dwelt among us, full of grace and truth" (1:14).

All this was written down in a number of books, the best of which were selected to become our Bible. And thus it is that God's speaking, God's word has come down to us in the Bible. It is better to put it this way than to say that the Bible is God's Word. The Bible contains the Word of God to man more clearly than anything else, but not equally in all its parts. For instance, compare Esther with the Gospel of John. The former never mentions God at all. The latter is the finest treatise ever written on Jesus and his meaning to both God and man. Or compare Exodus 21:23-24 with Matthew 5:38-39. The former says: "And if any mischief follow, then thou shalt give life for life. Eye for eye, tooth for tooth, hand for hand, foot for foot." That is revenge, pure and simple. But in the latter it is Jesus speaking: "You have heard that it was said, 'An eye for an eye and a tooth for a tooth.' But I say to you, Do not resist one who is evil. But if any one strikes you on the right cheek, turn to him the other also." People were slow to comprehend what God was saying. Or, to put it the other way around, God had to speak his truth slowly and patiently, as people could take it in. But in Jesus nothing was held back; here God said all that he had to say.

Some Bible Difficulties

The Bible is by no means an easy book to read, understand, and get help from.

To begin with, the various books were written at widely different periods of time, in the midst of many varied circumstances. In order to catch the full message of a given book, you almost have to understand what was happening at the time of its writing. For instance, you can get something just by picking up and reading Amos 5:21-24, in which God is represented as wanting from the Israelites not sacrifices of fat beasts, but fair treatment of one another. However, in order to get the full import of Amos' book, you need to know that Amos taught and wrote in an era of peace and prosperity for the Israelites; that this wealth was not distributed evenly, but some were in great need while others lived luxuriously; that the wealthy and powerful cheated and oppressed the poor at every turn; that Assyria to the northeast was on the march, but the Israelites thought God would protect them because

55

they were his people and because they offered him such nice sacrifices. If you have this background, you appreciate the book and catch its message far better. The same is true of many books of the Bible.

Furthermore, the Bible came out of a shepherd and farming civilization on the other side of the world two to three thousand years ago, and many of the customs referred to are strange to us. When the 23d Psalm speaks of anointing the head with oil, it means nothing to us unless we know that this was a way of being hospitable to a guest, somewhat like offering him a cup of tea nowadays. And when this same Psalm speaks of the Lord as a Shepherd tending his sheep, what can that mean to city-dwellers who never saw a shepherd and very few sheep? A policeman they understand but a shepherd scarcely at all.

A minor obstacle is the old English phraseology in many of our translations. "Verily, verily, I say unto you"—how strange that would sound in a high school classroom or gymnasium! However, modern translations are available, which put the Bible in present-day speech.

Besides all these, there is the difficulty that some things in the Bible perplex modern young people. Many strange and miraculous happenings are reported from time to time. We have already spoken of these in connection with Jesus, but they are present in the Old Testament as well. God covered the whole earth with a flood, saving only one family and representatives of the various species of animals (Genesis 6:5-9:17). God sent a succession of plagues to harass the Egyptians and persuade them to release the Israelites from bondage (Exodus 7-12). God went ahead of the Israelites in their desert wanderings in a pillar of cloud by day and a pillar of fire by night (Exodus 13:21-22). In a time of famine Elijah provided for a widow containers of meal and oil that never became empty, and also restored her stricken child to life (I Kings 17). Isaiah had a vision of the Lord, in which God said to him, "Whom shall I send, and who will go for us?"; and Isaiah answered, "Here am I; send me" (Isaiah 6). And many more!

Most Christians have accepted all of these as literal fact, exactly as they are reported. But there are others who are puzzled by such incidents. They don't see God acting in such a fashion today. They recall that some of these stories were repeated by word of mouth through many generations, and then written down a long time afterwards by people who had no notion of science such as we possess today. Further, they remind themselves that the writers of the Bible, being deeply religious, gave a religious turn to everything they said. Whereas we might say, "It rained this afternoon," they would be inclined to say, "The Lord sent rain upon the earth." Whereas we might say, "It seemed best for me to do thus and so," or, "I felt it was the Lord's will that I should do thus and so," they would come right out and say, "The Lord told me to do thus and so." Maybe they were nearer right than we are, at that.

Whatever you believe concerning the details of these narratives, the important thing is to catch the spiritual truth behind them. Behind the flood narrative lies the great truth that in the long run in God's world wickedness is punished and righteousness is rewarded; and so it is. Behind the account of the plagues lies the truth that God delivers his faithful people out of their afflictions; and so he does. Behind the strange story of the pillar of cloud by day and fire by night lies the profound truth that God is with his people wherever they go and whatever befalls them; and so he is. Behind the Elijah story lies the truth that Elijah was a man of God, who left behind him the reputation of being helpful to people in need; and so he was. Behind the vivid description of Isaiah's vision and call lies the undeniable fact that Isaiah drew close to the Lord, and was responsive to his will; and so he certainly was. It is not the details that matter chiefly; it is the spiritual truth behind and beneath them. And most of the Bible's abiding truth comes to us in passages that contain no difficulties of this sort at all. There is no possible conflict, for example, between the 23d Psalm and modern science. You can take the 23d Psalm in one hand, and a science textbook in the other, and the two will never get in each other's way.

Perhaps the chief thing to remember, whenever questions of this sort arise in your mind, is that the Bible was written in a pre-scientific age, by people who had no training in science and no interest in science. During the past century our geologists and biologists through study of rocks, fossils, and vegetable and animal species have arrived at the conclusion that the universe, including our world and the life upon it, took ages upon ages to reach its present form. Then you turn to the first chapter of Genesis and find an account of God creating all of it in six days. Now the point is that the writer of this chapter never had a course in science, and might not have cared much for it if one had been offered him. What he was interested in was religion. So, if you want to know how the world was made and how long it took, go to present-day scientists. They will give you the best available answer. But if you want to know who made the world and for what purpose it was made, go to the first chapter of Genesis. It will give you the best available answer. In the field of religion, which is its specialty, the Bible is still our supreme and unique textbook.

The Central Message of the Bible

The central message of the Bible, as we have just seen, does not lie in the field of science. If science is what you are after, turn to a laboratory or a modern scientific textbook.

The central message of the Bible does not lie in the field of history, although it contains much accurate history. If it is history you want, go to a professor or a book of history.

The central message of the Bible does not lie in the field of predicting what will happen next year or in the year 2007 A.D. If that is what you want to know, you had better give up the idea. The future rests with God, and with man's response to God's will. Some people have thought they found in occasional numbers or phrases references to Hitler or Russia, and on this basis have worked out a scheme of things to come. But the Bible was not intended for this purpose. It is probably just as well if we do not know what is going to happen to us and to the world.

The primary message of the Bible has to do with God. He is the major character. He is the hero of the Bible. A Concordance is a book which lists all the words, one by one, which occur in the Bible, and the passages in which they are found. The word "God" appears more than four thousand times in the pages of the Bible; and this does not include "Lord" or "Father" or any of the other names by which God is known. So there can be no doubt as to what the Bible is about. It is primarily about God. Slowly and patiently God revealed himself to men. Little by little they understood his true nature, and discerned his will. God was speaking, and men were listening. And the Bible writers wrote it down, for us and all men to read. Between the covers of this Book you will find more about God than anywhere else. Here is the tremendous story of his power, his majesty, his awful greatness, his will, his purposes for mankind, his love for us, his gracious provision for our every need, his forgiveness of our sins, his suffering with us in our sorrows, and his eventual triumph when sin and suffering shall be no more. This is the major theme of the Bible, running through its pages like a golden thread. The opening chapter of Genesis starts with the familiar words, "In the beginning God." And the last chapter of Revelation holds out before the eyes of hounded and persecuted Christians the vision of a heavenly realm in which their troubles will be forgotten and they will live in the joy of God's continual presence: "And night shall be no more; they need no light of lamp or sun, for the Lord God will be their light, and they shall reign for ever and ever" (Revelation 22:5). This is the first thing to be got from the Bible—its message concerning God.

The secondary message of the Bible has to do with us. As

the centuries rolled by, God kept telling men in all sorts of ways who they were, whence they had come, whither they were going, what they were destined to be, how they should live with one another, and how they ought to respond to his gracious dealings with them. They understood, partially at first, and more fully at the last. And the Bible writers wrote it down. Now it is contained in the pages of this Book for our guidance and inspiration. This is the minor theme of the Bible, running through its pages like a silver thread. From the Ten Commandments to the Sermon on the Mount the Bible tells us who we are, and what we can be with God's help. The first chapter of Genesis begins the story: "So God created man in his own image, in the image of God created he him" (Genesis 1:27). And the last chapter of Revelation brings it to a fitting and poetic close: "They shall see his face, and his name shall be on their foreheads" (Revelation 22:4). This is the second thing to be gotten from the Bible—its message concerning man.

One more thing remains to be said in this connection: in a very real sense Jesus himself is the central message of the whole Bible. In him it reaches its climax. In him it is all summed up. In a complete and final revelation or "unveiling" he both tells us and shows us what God is. And he also tells us and shows us what we are and can become. The four Gospels, while they do not stand in the middle of the Bible but come at a point three-fourths through its pages, are in reality the living heart of the Book. They give us Jesus. They are the most valuable books in all literature. The part which follows—The Acts, the Epistles, and Revelation—describes the experiences which men had of Jesus, the meaning which he held for them and the world, and the Church which grew up around him. The part which precedes—the Old Testament—leads up to him and prepares the way for him. Notice how the book of Hebrews opens: "In many and various ways God spoke of old to our fathers by the prophets; but in these last days he has spoken to us by a Son." This earlier speaking was necessary to prepare men's minds and hearts for Jesus. Without it they might not have known who he was and what he meant. So Jesus himself is the Bible's central message.

When you turn to the Bible, then, make sure what it is you are looking for, or you may not find it. And whatever else you seek, try to lay hold on the person and spirit of Jesus. He is the "A" and the "Z," the beginning and the end, the first and the last.

Can You Hear God Speak?

There is no point in God's speaking in the Bible, if you and I do not hear him.

When you are in doubt as to what is right and what is wrong, turn to the Ten Commandments (Deuteronomy 5), or to the Sermon on the Mount (Matthew 5, 6, and 7), and see if he says anything to you through these pages.

If sickness or death comes near you, turn to the opening verses of John 14, and look for a message of comfort.

If you begin to worry about another world war and the future of our civilization, turn to the picture of a new heaven and a new earth in Revelation 21:1-7. Perhaps this hope will encourage you, as it did the early Christians.

When you have done something wrong and are overwhelmed by a sense of guilt and worthlessness, turn to the 32nd Psalm. Does it help you to hold your head up, and try again?

If you fall to wondering what is of chief importance in the Christian life—going to church, singing in the choir, giving money generously, keeping the Sabbath, memorizing Bible verses, or something else—turn to Paul's poem on Christian love in I Corinthians 13. Does this serve to clear the matter up at all?

This is one way of gaining help from the Bible, namely, to go to it with a specific problem or purpose in mind.

Another way is to open it to some especially fine passage, and read it with a view to seeing what it has to say to you.

61

Romans 12 would be good, or Psalm 46, or many other portions that could be mentioned.

You can follow this same plan with an entire book, although now the task becomes harder and you really need some collateral reading such as a one-volume commentary. Your pastor can suggest a good one, or even lend you one of his own. The book of Amos is quite short, only nine chapters. But in order to get the most from it, you should know when it was written and what was going on in Israel at the time (as has been pointed out earlier). Then you should be able to picture Amos himself, a self-contained desert shepherd, who every now and then went into the cities nearby to market his produce, and was shocked by the conditions he found there until he could keep quiet no longer. A novel like Dorothy Clarke Wilson's *The Herdsman* will enable you to picture both Amos and his times, until they are as real to you as your next door neighbor. At various places in the book you will come upon strange names and references which will not mean a thing to you unless you look them up in a commentary. All of this takes some time, but at the close you will not only be familiar with the book of Amos but will also have got hold of some bits of eternal truth.

Similar study is useful with the four Gospels, but not quite so essential. Matthew, Mark, Luke, and John can be read at any time, and they will never let you down.

The Bible is worthless so long as it remains a closed book on a table or desk. It comes alive only as we open it and read it understandingly and appreciatively, looking always for what God said to people long ago and what he has to say to us today.

5

I will build my church.
—MATTHEW 16: 18

THE CHURCH OF CHRIST

I love Thy Church, O God:
Her walls before Thee stand,
Dear as the apple of Thine eye,
And graven on Thy hand.

For her my tears shall fall,
For her my prayers ascend;
To her my cares and toils be given,
Till toils and cares shall end.

Beyond my highest joy
I prize her heavenly ways,
Her sweet communion, solemn vows,
Her hymns of love and praise.

—TIMOTHY DWIGHT
*American educator and
author,* 1752-1817.

WHAT do you see when you look at your home church? It may be a small, one-room chapel. Or it may be a mighty, cathedral-like edifice. It may sit quietly beside a country road with only the sounds of birds and bees to disturb the stillness. Or it may crouch in the midst of the constant turmoil and towering buildings of a down-town city street. There are several hundred thousand like it in the United States alone, and countless others around the world. What do you see in it?

Do you see primarily a building—roof, walls, floor, windows, pulpit, organ? It is that, of course; and good buildings are highly necessary for the work of the Church. But for many years the Early Church existed and grew without any buildings of its own, meeting in homes, in the catacombs, or wherever Christians could assemble. Today a certain sect, a branch of the Amish, has no churches, but its members meet in houses and barns for worship.

Do you see primarily a group of people banding themselves together in a club somewhat like Rotary or Kiwanis, except that this is a religious club? This is one way of viewing the Church, and there is a measure of truth in it. For if people did not voluntarily give themselves to the Church, it could not continue. But this is not the whole truth. It may not even be the bigger half of the truth.

There is another way of viewing the Church.

The Body of Christ

From the earliest days of Christian history, the Church has been thought of as the body of Christ. A letter written by St. Paul long ago to a group of Christians states this idea plainly. Read, if you will, I Corinthians 12:12-27, remembering that it was written only about twenty years after the Church began. The first and last verses give the gist of it: "For just as the body is one and has many members, and all the members of the body, though many, are one body, so it is with Christ. . . . Now you are the body of Christ and individually members of it."

This is a most useful way of viewing the Church.

The important thing about a body is the life or spirit within it. John Jones's body contains John Jones within it. John Jones is the significant thing about it. Take John Jones out of it, and it isn't worth a great deal. Its main task is to transport John Jones where he wants to go, and to carry out what John Jones wants to accomplish; in other words, to be his servant. So is it with the Church. The most important thing about the Church is the spirit of Christ within it. Take Jesus' spirit out of it, and it isn't worth a great deal. Its main

64

task is to carry out what Jesus wants to accomplish; in other words, to continue the work which he began during the short years of his ministry.

A body has many members—eyes, ears, nose, arms, legs, stomach, lungs. In the same way, the Church has many members—individuals, congregations, even denominations. For we are thinking of the Church in the broadest possible terms. It is a world-wide fellowship of Christians, including people of every race, nation, and continent. You and I are members of this universal Church, as the eyes are members of the body. Our local congregations are all members of this body. Still larger members are the various denominations, of which there are more than two hundred in the United States alone. The many members differ widely one from another, but the spirit of Jesus dwells in every part of this far-flung organism. It has been kept alive in hymns, preaching, prayer, stained-glass windows, and earnest Christian living. After all, we today are only sixty generations removed from the time when Jesus was alive on the earth.

You can see now why it is not enough to think of the Church merely as bricks and stone, or as a religious club or society. It is a body in which Jesus continues to live on indefinitely. It is the extension of Jesus' spirit, Jesus' life, Jesus' work in the world. As such, God probably counts on it heavily for the carrying out of his purposes for the more than two billions of people on the earth. If Jesus held a special importance in God's plan, so must the Church. Here is the best place for children and young people to come to know about him, and find out what he would have them do—not the only place, but the best place. Here is an especially good starting-point for waves of influence, which will spread into community life and finally throughout the world, tearing down hate and injustice and wickedness of every sort.

Jesus' first body lived on this earth only some thirty-five years. His second body, the Church, still continues to live and grow. Because this figure of speech is so helpful in our thinking about the Church, we shall carry it with us through this chapter.

Some Things the Church Does

A body performs many functions or activities, such as eating, breathing, digesting, working, and the like. In the same way the Church, as the body of Christ, has different functions and carries on different activities. The ones named in the following list have stood out most prominently during the Church's history.

1. *The administration of the sacraments.* From the very first year of the Church's existence, the sacraments have held a leading place in its life. In time the Roman Catholic Church developed seven, including marriage, confirmation, and others which we Protestants do not regard as sacraments. Protestants generally hold to two only, Baptism and Communion, or the Lord's Supper. A sacrament may be simply defined as a sacred and symbolic act, traceable to Jesus, which sets forth in an object lesson great truths of our Christian faith.

Let us look first at Baptism in this light. The sacred symbolism used here is that of cleansing by water. Baptism can be traced clearly to Jesus, because he himself was baptized by John the Baptist at the river Jordan. And what are the great truths which it sets forth? Here are some for you to think about the next time you see a father and mother bring their child to the minister to be baptized (the meanings are somewhat different when a young person or adult is baptized):

God is willing to forgive our sins, and make us clean and pure.

God desires to claim every child as his own.

The Church welcomes each new life into its fellowship.

Every baby has untold possibilities of growth and Christian service.

Parents have the duty to bring up their child in the Christian faith and the Christian way of life.

Turn now to Communion or the Lord's Supper. Here the

sacred symbols are bread and wine, representing the broken body and the shed blood of our Lord's crucifixion. This too can be traced to Jesus, because he gathered the disciples in a Last Supper the night before he was put to death, giving them bread to eat and wine to drink. And what are the great truths which it sets forth? Here are some for you to think about the next time you take communion:

Jesus loved people to the point of being willing to have his body broken and his blood shed on the cross.

God cares for us always the way Jesus cared for us those six hours on the cross.

We should be thankful to God for his great goodness to us.

We are in close fellowship with one another, and with all Christians in every land in every age who are united around one common table in one common faith.

We are in close association with Jesus, who is still alive, and is present in spirit as the host at the Supper, as he was the host that night in Jerusalem.

We reconsecrate ourselves to Jesus, and to God's service.

2. *The preaching of the Word.* Strictly speaking, this was not emphasized until the Protestant Reformation in the sixteenth century. In fact, during the Middle Ages there were few copies of the Bible, little reading of it, and little preaching from it. Then about four hundred years ago the Protestant reformers became dissatisfied with the Church of their day in Europe, which was the Roman Catholic Church. They felt that the Church they knew was partially smothering the spirit of Jesus, instead of keeping it alive and expressing it. So they did the natural thing—they turned directly to the Bible with its unchanging record of Jesus. Martin Luther made a fresh translation of the Bible into German; Ulrich Zwingli in Switzerland began a series of sermons on key books of the Bible, such as the Gospel of Matthew. From that day to this, the preaching of the Word has been regarded as one of the most important things the Church could do. In the average Protestant church service, from one-third to one-half of the

time is given over to a sermon, based generally on the Bible. Theological seminaries in their training of young men for the Christian ministry devote many hours to instruction in how to preach. The more you think about it, the more reasonable it seems; for the Bible is in a peculiar sense the Word of God to man (as we saw in our last chapter), and needs to be kept before us constantly.

3. *Worship.* During the greater part of the past nineteen hundred years, church people worshiped God principally through the Lord's Supper. Even today the regular form of worship in Roman Catholicism is the Mass. With the coming of the Protestant Reformation, our ancestors limited the Lord's Supper to comparatively few times a year. For the other Sundays they developed the kind of service with which we are familiar—hymns, scripture, prayer, a sermon. Nowadays the typical church offers us many opportunities to worship, not only in the church service, but also in church school, youth fellowship, and the like.

Have you ever made an appointment to meet a friend at a certain time and place? That is what worship is. It is meeting God at an appointed time and place. We do not go to church to hear the sopranos hit high "F" with precision, nor to listen to a sermon that is a literary masterpiece (although both of these can help the cause somewhat). We go to church to meet God face to face. When you go to church next Sunday, you will find a place made ready for this one purpose. Reminders of God will be there, a painting, a stained-glass window, a cross on the altar. Other people will be there with the same purpose. Out of the past will come hymns, scripture, prayer, a creed perhaps, in which Christians of former generations expressed their faith in God. Here you can forget for a little while the things that are seen, and center your thoughts on him who is unseen and eternal. God is there too. He will keep the appointment, if you do. Nothing miraculous will happen to you during the service. But when it is over, you will return home with God a little more real to you than he was

68

when you came, or than he would have been if you had stayed home to read the Sunday papers. You will be better, stronger, more able to meet life well during the coming week. Worship has always been, and will always be one of the most important things the Church does.

4. *Education.* The Church has been engaged in the business of education for a long time. A beginning was made during the early centuries when converts to Christianity were gathered into classes to be instructed in the "secrets" of this new faith. During the Middle Ages there was little formal education of any sort, but such as there was came largely from the Church, in the form of schools which grew up around cathedrals and monasteries. With the Reformation new catechisms were written, and classes were held once more to instruct prospective church members in the main items of the Christian faith.

Then in 1780—very few years ago as time runs—Robert Raikes started the first Sunday school in Gloucester, England. From this sprang a movement which has been taken up by the Church, changed considerably, and greatly expanded. At the end of 1947, according to statistics compiled by the International Council of Religious Education, there were almost thirty million pupils in the Sunday church schools (Protestant, Roman Catholic, and Jewish) of the United States. In addition, there were almost four million pupils in the vacation church schools of our country. Weekday classes of religion have grown rapidly in recent years, until they include a couple of million pupils at least. The Church is conducting academies, colleges, and seminaries in every land. It is preparing films, slides, and records; publishing books; holding summer camps and conferences; and issuing untold millions of lesson materials of various sorts; not to mention radio and television programs. The Church today is one of the foremost educators of the world.

5. *Missions and evangelism.* The Church has never been content so long as there were people outside its fellowship,

people who were not true members of the body of Christ. Beginning with a little handful of people around Jerusalem, this fellowship spread in the Mediterranean world, then farther afield into Europe and Asia, and then to the New World when it was finally discovered. This "growing edge" of the Church we call missions and evangelism. In our own land it is home missions and evangelism; in foreign lands it is missions.

The Church has not been equally interested in missions in every age, but it never forgot this great task for many years at a time. Did you know that Christian missionaries reached China eight hundred and fifty years before Columbus discovered America? We cannot begin to tell here the story of Christian missions century by century, but it is a great story. Suddenly around 1800, after a lull of some years, the Church burst forth into a new missionary enthusiasm. Since then the movement has grown by leaps and bounds. Time and again during World War II our soldiers in far-off corners of the earth stumbled upon people who had been Christianized by representatives of the Church. Modern missions now includes preaching, teaching, healing, agriculture, social reform—about anything and everything that the Christian spirit can devise to meet the needs of people.

Evangelism has often been linked in our minds with Billy Sunday and great revival meetings in tents or tabernacles. But it is far more than this. "Evangel" means "gospel" or good news; so evangelism includes every possible means of bringing people under the spell of the good news of God's love, made known to us in Jesus. Nowadays it often takes the form of a community survey, and friendly visits to unreached people in their homes to bring youth into youth groups, men into men's groups, and women into women's groups in the Church. At the present time there is renewed interest in evangelism on every hand, partly because of the realization that half the people of the United States are outside the Church.

6. *Social action.* From the earliest times Christianity has been concerned not only about each individual soul, but also about the customs and practices, good or bad, in the midst of which people have to live. The Early Church stopped the practice of killing newborn babies, cleaned up the indecent shows of the Roman theatre, and checked the cruel custom of setting gladiators to fighting and killing one another while the spectators applauded. It accomplished these things not so much by organized effort as by silent influence.

However, it has been only within the past century that the Church has taken seriously its task of helping people to be good by giving them a good world to live in. Today people rather generally expect the Church to have something to say and to do about unwholesome amusements, tension between races, unfair economic conditions, war and peace, and the like. One instance must suffice of this very important function of the Church. Several decades ago a twelve-hour day was normal in the steel industry of America. Workers had little home life, and were often so tired they scarcely cared to live. On May 25, 1923 a committee of the industry reported that nothing could be done about the matter. On June 6 a joint statement was released by Protestant, Roman Catholic, and Jewish agencies, which made the headlines. On July 6 a leader of the steel industry announced that they were determined to get rid of the twelve-hour day at the earliest possible moment.

7. *Brotherly service.* Last but not least, the Church helps those in need, in the name and in the spirit of Jesus. This activity, too, is of long standing. In the Early Church, offerings were taken regularly in each congregation for the care of widows and orphans. During the Dark Ages the Church took the lead in establishing hospitals.

At the close of World War II there were more people sick, more people hungry, more people cold, more people homeless, more people in prisons and concentration camps than the world had ever seen before. The Church began to mobilize

71

its resources on a grand scale. Money, food, clothing, and medicine were sent out through Church World Service and other agencies to the distressed people of Europe and Asia, some of them our late enemies. And a plan was set up to bring displaced persons to America to live. All this too is an inescapable part of the work of the Church.

Is the Church Perfect?

A body is generally imperfect. It doesn't do all that the spirit within it wants it to do. For many years athletes have been trying to run a hundred yards in nine seconds, and a mile in four minutes. But at the time this is being written, these goals have not yet been reached. The spirit is anxious, but the body is weak. Many a body limps along painfully, sees poorly, hears with difficulty; and every body is imperfect.

So is the Church, the body of Christ. Every now and then someone begins to point out defects within the Church. There are many of them. The individual members of the body are not always what they ought to be. They are sometimes selfish, proud, timid, short-sighted, and spiteful toward one another. And the Church itself is not always what it ought to be. It is sometimes slow to take up the tasks that belong to it. During the first three hundred years of Protestantism, for example, the Church did little along the line of missions. It is frequently slow to attack serious social evils. It often behaves like a chameleon, taking its color from its environment, instead of from Jesus. If a certain area practices slavery, the churches in that area are quite likely to approve of slavery. If a nation goes to war, the nation's churches generally give their blessing to the war.

And yet, the Church still has within it the spirit of Jesus, reminding it constantly of what it ought to be. And it keeps on trying to be faithful to that spirit. Over the years it has done more to change individuals, help those in need, and improve social conditions than any other institution on the earth. During World War II the Church succeeded in staying more or less above the battle. Its leaders often criticized a nation, including their own, when they felt it was doing something particularly inhuman. And British and American money helped to keep German missions going during the war and afterwards. In Germany the Church stood out more boldly against totalitarianism than the universities, the labor unions, or any other force. It was this fact which turned the great mathematician, Einstein, from a critic into an admirer of the Church.

Yes, the Church, the body of Christ, is imperfect. But the spirit within it is not imperfect. Compared with that spirit, it is not as yet what it ought to be. Compared with other institutions, it is the best this world has seen.

Being a Good Member of the Church

A member of a body must do two things: first, it must stay in close touch with the body as a whole; and, secondly, it must do its part in the body. We as members of the Church have exactly these same two responsibilities.

If an ear, a finger, or an arm is cut off from the body, it soon becomes a useless piece of flesh and decays. The life of the body is no longer coursing through it. Occasionally we hear someone say, "I can be just as good a Christian outside the Church as in it." Maybe he can, but the chances are he can't. Ninety-nine out of a hundred can't. The Church has something we need. It is older than we are. It is greater than we are. It is the "carrier" of the spirit of Jesus in a special sense. We may think we can get along as well without the Church as with it, but we are probably wrong. Sometimes young people drift away from the Church, because they have lost interest in it momentarily, or have other interests, or go away to college, or take a job in another community. You run a heavy risk if you allow yourself to be cut off from the Church for any length of time.

The task of each member of a body is not to advance its own interests, or to attract attention to itself, but to serve the

73

body as a whole. The purpose of the eye is not to make people say, "Oh, what a beautiful eye!" but to help the whole body to see. The purpose of the hand is to help the whole body run a machine, or play the piano. So is it with us as members of the Church. Each of us has his task to perform. Perhaps our part is merely to stand by the Church with our attendance and financial support. Or it may be to sing in the choir, to usher, or to teach in the church school. It may even be to become a minister, a missionary, or a director of religious education. Whatever it is, we should do it as faithfully as possible. If we fail, the whole body is weakened. If we do our part, the whole body is strengthened.

There are many worthy ambitions which a young person may set for his or her life. Among them, this is not the least: "I will be a good member of the Church."

6

If a man die, shall he live again?
—JOB 14: 14

IF A MAN DIE—

Abide with me: fast falls the eventide;
The darkness deepens; Lord, with me abide:
When other helpers fail, and comforts flee,
Help of the helpless, O abide with me.

Swift to its close ebbs out life's little day;
Earth's joys grow dim, its glories pass away;
Change and decay in all around I see;
O Thou who changest not, abide with me.

I fear no foe, with Thee at hand to bless:
Ills have no weight, and tears no bitterness.
Where is death's sting? Where, grave, thy victory?
I triumph still, if Thou abide with me.

—HENRY FRANCIS LYTE
Scottish curate, 1793-1847.

YOUNG people, as a rule, do not think about death a great deal. It is right that they should not, for in the normal course of events they have many years remaining to live on this earth. Death is as yet unreal, something that happens to other people, and in other families, but not to them. There will be plenty of time for them to face up realistically to the fact of death.

And yet it may well be that we make too little of death in our teaching and thinking nowadays. There was a time when religious instruction constantly reminded even little children that they were moving slowly but surely toward the end of life, and an awful judgment beyond. Now we have swung to

75

the opposite extreme, and almost pretended that there is no such thing as death.

Sooner or later, death comes close to each of us, either in our own persons, or in those to whom we are deeply attached. What then? What, if anything, lies beyond?

Wishful Thinking?

Ever since man has been man, he has fought against the idea that death is the end, and clung wistfully to the hope of immortality. Long before primitive man could read or write, he got the idea of a soul separate from the body. Perhaps this notion came to him first as a result of his dreams. We can see easily how this could be. In a dream he was stalking a wild animal skilfully through the forest, pouncing upon it bravely with his stone club, and then returning in triumph with food for his family slung over his shoulder. But when he woke up, he found himself not hunting at all but merely taking a nap in his cave. The whole experience must have puzzled him greatly. One likely explanation was that his body had remained in the cave, but his spirit had gone out hunting. Or conceivably this notion first struck him on the occasion of the death of a brave chieftain. Here was a man who a few hours ago had been very much alive, leading the clan into the hunt or into battle, and respected and feared by all. Now he lay motionless and harmless. Obviously something had gone out of him. Perhaps it was the life, the breath, the spirit, which continued its own existence apart from the body.

However the notion came to our remote ancestors, it reached them a long time ago. Present-day scholars, digging down through the layers of bygone civilizations, come upon the bones of a grown man or a little child, surrounded by vessels and objects that the dead person was thought to need in the life beyond. Here is silent and touching evidence that the people of that distant period believed death was not the end.

In nations like China ancestor worship has been practiced for thousands of years. The Chinese have long believed that

76

when a person dies his soul is still very much alive. It can move around virtually at will, but its chief dwelling-places are two in number. The one is the grave where the body is buried. The other is the ancestor-tablet, two thin pieces of wood perhaps a foot high and several inches wide, fitted neatly together and set upright on a base. All significant events in the living family are faithfully reported to the ancestor, and ceremonies of worship are offered regularly to his spirit. Here is more evidence of the ancient belief in continued life after death.

Is all of this mere wishful thinking? Have our forefathers been mistaken these countless years? Has God allowed us to cherish this hope, when all the while there was nothing to it? Are we mistaken today in our beliefs concerning immortality?

Psychology Doesn't Help

If you have not done so already, one of these days you may find yourself reading or studying psychology. In it you will learn that the nervous system, including the brain and spinal cord, is made up of myriads of nerve cells and long nerve fibers. Branching out from the cell bodies and from the tips of the fibers are tiny tendrils, which interlace with other tendrils from other cell bodies and fibers. Out on the edge of our bodies are eyes and ears, nose, taste-buds, and tiny centers for registering pressure, temperature, and pain. From these sense organs, impulses flash in to the central part of the nervous system, the spinal cord and brain. In this center, the messages are cleared and woven into a pattern. Then impulses stream out again to stomach, heart, glands, and muscles.

Here, psychology seems to tell us, is where "we" live. In and through this marvelous nervous system we think, feel, purpose, and act. And there seems to be much truth to this point of view. Damage the eye or the optic nerve, and we can no longer see. Crush or tear a main motor-nerve to a leg, and we are paralyzed and cannot walk. Destroy some of the brain tissue in an automobile accident, or even strike the skull a severe blow, and the victim may lie for weeks in a coma, not knowing that he is alive. As a matter of fact, it looks as though only the body were alive, while "he" himself is not there.

Now all of this doesn't help us to believe in immortality. It seems to suggest that what we call personal life is dependent upon this nervous system. When it is alive, "we" live. When it dies, "we" die. More than one student of psychology has found greater and greater difficulty, the more psychology he studied, in holding fast to the Christian faith in immortality. A young minister once plunged into a year's work at a university in which he devoted himself partly to psychology. In the spring he had to preach an Easter sermon at a church. A great deal of wrestling in mind and conscience was required before he could find something positive to say to the people who came to church that bright Easter morning.

But let us not jump to conclusions too quickly. Psychology seems to have established beyond reasonable doubt that there is a close relation between this nervous system and personality, or the soul, or whatever you want to call it. But the question still remains, Which is primary and which secondary? No psychologist has yet proved conclusively that the nervous system "makes" personality, so that when the nerve cells and fibers die, personality dies with them. Indeed, the situation may be just the other way around. It may be just as true or truer to say that personality uses the nervous system, as to say that the nervous system generates personality. To illustrate these two points of view, we may compare a dynamo and an electric motor. Electricity is present in both. But in the one case, electricity is generated by the dynamo. When the dynamo stops turning, there is no more electricity. In the other case, electricity uses the motor to get things done. Conceivably the motor is a better illustration of the relation between personality and nervous system, between soul and body, than the dynamo. If so, the nervous system could deteriorate and die, but the person who has used it for a while could live on.

In recent years psychology itself has brought forth some hard-and-fast evidence pointing in this direction. At Duke University and in other psychological research centers, a great deal of experimentation has been done with extra-sensory perception, more commonly called "mental telepathy." The device most often used has been a deck of twenty-five cards, containing five with wavy lines, five with squares, five with stars, five with circles, and five with crosses. Two experimenters work together. Experimenter No. 1 turns over these shuffled cards one by one, but says nothing. Experimenter No. 2 tries to read the other's mind and discern what card he is seeing and thinking of at the moment. The two persons have sometimes sat across a table from each other, and sometimes have been separated by hundreds of miles, communicating by telephone. By sheer chance, a person will make an average of five right answers in a deck of twenty-five cards. But in hundreds of experiments, some people have averaged seven or eight right answers consistently. One person averaged eighteen correct answers in seventy-four times through the deck. This is the sort of thing that simply doesn't happen by chance. That is inconceivable. The only scientific conclusion is that two persons can within limits communicate with each other above and beyond the usual methods of sight, sound, and touch. Person is meeting person directly and immediately—not by means of the bodies that both possess. It begins to look, then, as though personal life had some rights of its own. Personal life is not utterly dependent upon the body in which it dwells. It may be just as true to say that it uses the body, as to say that it is created by the body. Conceivably, then, when the body dies, the person can find a way of continuing to live on.

The net result of this little excursion into psychology may well be the conclusion that psychology makes it hard but not impossible for us to believe in immortality. Some psychological findings tend to suggest that faith in immortality is not so unreasonable after all. But the main support for our belief at this point is not to be found in present-day psychology. For that we must turn elsewhere.

The Christian Faith Does Help

Christians have two main grounds for their hope of immortality. These two are not separate, but are really one.

For nineteen hundred years we have taken comfort from the conviction that Jesus was victorious over death, and that we shall be also. St. Paul phrased this conviction in words that endure: "O death, where is thy victory? O death, where is thy sting? The sting of death is sin, and the power of sin is the law. But thanks be to God, who gives us the victory through our Lord Jesus Christ" (I Corinthians 15:55-57).

You can search the Old Testament from start to finish, and find little concerning immortality. The biblical quotation at the head of this chapter is from the book of Job in the Old Testament, but it merely states a question: "If a man die, shall he live again?" The Christians of the New Testament had the answer, and it was "Yes." It is to be found on almost every page of the New Testament. In this radiant hope the first Christians lived, suffered, and died. It carried over into the later persecutions, and followers of Jesus often welcomed death because of their faith that continued life lay beyond, a life far better than their present existence. It has come down to our own day undiminished.

All this had its origin in the conviction that Jesus had proved conqueror over every enemy of the human spirit, including the last great enemy, death. It started within a few days of Jesus' crucifixion, and it never let up. Christianity has been called the only world religion that had its source in a belief in immortality. And it does make sense to go back to Jesus for our faith in this regard. If a person like him could be brought to an end after only thirty-five years, there isn't much chance for us. If he is alive forevermore, there is ground for believing that we too shall live.

But in the final analysis, our chief reason for daring to be-

lieve in immortality is our faith in God. We might as well
say this once and for all. Even when we make Jesus our
starting-point, we are harking back to God, for it is "God,
who gives us the victory through our Lord Jesus Christ." If
Jesus is still alive, that very fact tells us something about God,
something on which we too can depend.

We begin with the faith that God is our Father, and we are
his children. If he is our Father, then he cares for us. And if
he truly cares for us, his concern lasts not just a little while
but always. We can say of him as has been said of Jesus: "Having loved his own . . . he loved them to the end." Then
nothing, not even death, can take us out of the Father's house
or beyond the reach of his continuous care. It would be a
rather heartless Father who would make us in his own image,
rear us into self-conscious sons and daughters, develop in us
personalities capable of thinking high thoughts and planning
noble deeds, permit us to dream dreams of a life that has no
end—and then after a very few years snuff us out as one blows
out a candle. If we are deceived concerning him, and he is
really not a loving Father, then we have little reason to hope
for immortality. But if he is what we have believed him to be,
then the age-old Christian hope rests on a sure foundation. It
is still not a proven fact; it is faith, but faith sure enough to
live by and to die by.

A man who had lived his entire life within the Church
reached his eightieth birthday recently. At a dinner given him
on that occasion, he arose and said: "In my long life I have
had many exciting adventures. I have crossed the ocean
numerous times, and have been around the world. But I am
awaiting now the greatest adventure of all, the journey into
that land from which no traveler has ever returned." That is
the sort of faith with which a Christian faces the end of this
life.

The point just made—that God cares for us deeply, and
therefore we may venture to believe he will care for us to the
end—can be said in somewhat different words, using the

language of science instead of the language of religion. The fossils of the rocks and the various vegetable and animal species tell a story of countless ages devoted to the process of evolution. This process seems to be going somewhere. It looks as though it had a purpose. The end result of it all is man, human personality. In other words, our universe has lavished endless time and patience on the production of what we call personality. Does it make sense, then, to suppose that the universe after all this effort would suddenly turn around and blot out its most delicate creation? If you watched a skilled craftsman spending twenty years in fashioning a particularly fine watch, would you expect him to let it run five minutes and then crush it to bits under his heel?

Some people find consolation in the thought that, even if individual persons do not live on, personality itself continues, in that parents have children and they have other children and so the process goes on and on. But, sooner or later, this world of ours is likely to become a cold, blackened cinder, unable any longer to support life. Sooner or later, then, the last generation will come to an end, and the last person on earth will die. When that happens man's noble experiment on this planet will be over. And what will it have amounted to? Exactly nothing! No, this way of thinking merely postpones for a few million years the day when it will become clear that this universe doesn't make sense.

But our universe does make sense. All along the line it acts as though it were "up to something." And if it has gone to so much trouble to create personality, it is likely to take lasting care of what it has made. The religious way is still the best way of saying it: If God loves us, he will love us to the end.

What Is the Future Like?

If there is a life on the other side of what we call death, what will it be like? Where are we going to spend eternity? What kind of bodies, if any, shall we have? How shall we put in our time?

Fortunately, we don't have to bother too much about questions such as these. Jesus himself was rather indefinite concerning the whole matter. Toward the end of his earthly life, when Jesus was trying to prepare the disciples for his separation from them for a while, he said, "Let not your heart be troubled; believe in God, believe also in me. In my Father's house are many rooms" (John 14:1-2). That is really all that we need to know. This present life is one room in the Father's house. The life beyond is another room in the same house. We don't need to know precisely where that room is, or what it looks like, or the kind of furniture it will contain. All we need to know is that it is a part of the Father's house, and his love and care are in control there as they are here. The rest we can leave to him for the present; and some day we shall find out for ourselves.

Many people probably don't think any longer of a heaven of golden streets and pearly gates up above the sky, or a hell of fire and brimstone down below the earth. For one thing, now that we know our earth is a planet spinning around on its axis, there is no longer any "up" or "down." Furthermore, such a heaven is designed to please bodies, and such a hell is made to punish bodies. But if in the future life we don't have bodies, or at least bodies like the ones we now live in, there would be little satisfaction in golden streets and little pain in endless fire. You can't very well burn a spirit. There is something to be said for picturing the life beyond in spiritual terms, rather than in bodily terms.

This is not to say that there will be no judgment, and no rewards or punishments awaiting us. Indeed, we are being judged all the while, and the rewards and punishments can be seen even now. Every day is Judgment Day.

Imagine a man completely wrapped up in himself. All he can think about is himself, his aches and pains, his petty successes, the impression he is making on other people. The doors of his life to fellowship with other people and with God are closed. He has nothing big and interesting to live for. A man wrapped up in himself, as a church bulletin board once said, makes a pretty small package; and he gets smaller and smaller as the years go on. He is unhappy now, and he will become more and more unhappy. He is in hell now; and his life will become more hellish during the remainder of his days on this earth, and during the eternity beyond (unless he changes somewhere along the line).

Imagine also a man living only for his body. The things that make life worth while to him are steak dinners and cocktails. But as he grows older, his body wears out. He can't eat so many steak dinners, nor drink so many cocktails. And all he gets from them is indigestion and inflammation of the liver. He is following a blind alley, leading nowhere. And what will it be like when he wakes up some morning without this body? Nothing to live for! Nothing to give life meaning! If that isn't hell, what is it? We begin to see the truth of the penetrating statement that the problem of heaven is how to be happy without a stomach.

Imagine now another man of a different sort. He may live on the same block as these others, speak the same language, wear the same kind of clothes. But this man is not overly concerned about himself. He is interested in his family, and his neighbors. He thinks a good deal about underprivileged groups in this country, and people in dire need on other continents. He takes an active part in his church and the affairs of his community. He "gets a kick" out of his job. The doors of his soul are open to God, who becomes more and more real to him as the years pass. He takes proper care of his body, but he doesn't depend too much on the pleasure it can give him. Instead, he derives real satisfaction from good literature, art, and music. Such a man is quite happy now. He will be happier at seventy than he is at forty. And when he is called upon to lay aside this body, he can keep right on going with increasing happiness; for he has built his life on the joys of the spirit rather than the satisfactions of the body. In other words, he is, and will be, in heaven.

Many believe, then, that in the world beyond we shall continue to live, to learn, and to grow in fellowship with God and man. Some who have resisted God's will and held out against his love may in twenty or thirty thousand years give in and yield themselves to his gracious purposes. Those who have made a good start may keep on in the same direction, and find in ever increasing measure the joys which God has intended for his children.

Some visitors once paid a call upon a remarkable old man. He had been a leading figure in his community, serving as principal of the high school and mayor of the city. He had also been something of an athlete. Over in one corner still stood the weights and pulleys which he had used to develop his muscles. But now his body was failing fast. He sat in a wheel chair, and gazed steadily at his callers from eyes set deep beneath a massive shock of white hair. Quite naturally and peacefully he spoke about the approach of death. He was eager to take this step, he said, and for two reasons. He was anxious to meet his wife, who had died some years before, and whom he had not seen for quite a while. Besides, he had always been deeply interested in astronomy. Once he was freed from the limitations of his ailing body, he thought he might find out something about some distant stars which had always been a mystery to him. He has long since died, as this is written. There is satisfaction in the thought that he now may be closer to his wife than ever before, and that he may have found out about those distant stars.

There is, then, nothing for Christians to worry about in death. Perhaps there is something ahead finer than we can dream of. If a lowly caterpillar could talk, as he makes his tedious way over twigs and stones, he would ridicule the idea that before long he will be a many-colored butterfly flying easily from flower to flower. But we know that this will happen. A like change may lie ahead for us, though we are hard to convince. God knows about it. He will take care of the matter. We are in his hands, both now and forever.

7

*Thy kingdom come, thy will be done, on earth
as it is in heaven.*

—MATTHEW 6: 10

THY KINGDOM COME

O thou King eternal, immortal, invisible, the only wise
God, our Savior; hasten, we beseech thee, the coming of thy
kingdom upon earth, and draw the whole world of mankind
into willing obedience to thy blessed reign. Overcome all
the enemies of Christ, and bring low every power that is
exalted against him. Cast out all the evil things which cause
wars and fighting among us, and let thy Spirit rule the
hearts of men in righteousness and love. Restore what was
made desolate in former days; let the wilderness rejoice
with beauty; and make glad the city with thy law. Estab-
lish every work that is founded on truth and equity, and
fulfill all the good hopes and desires of mankind. Manifest
thy will, Almighty Father, in the brotherhood of man, and
bring in universal peace; through the victory of Christ our
Lord. Amen.

Book of Worship, *the Evangelical
and Reformed Church.*

SOME words are deceptive. They seem so simple, until we
try to define them. Take the word "yellow," for example.
You have used it all your life. You know what it means, of
course. But now try to define it. In what respects is it different
from red or blue? What makes a yellow rose yellow? And
how can we tell that it is yellow? How would you go at it to
make this word clear to a person blind from birth? Or take a
still shorter word, "up." Everybody knows what "up" means.
But as a matter of fact, it points in one direction in the United

States, and in another direction in China. In New York it is the opposite at noon from what it is at midnight. At the North Pole, on the contrary, it remains constant. What, after all, does "up" mean?

The word "kingdom," as Christians use it, belongs to this same class of words. Every time you repeat the Lord's Prayer, you say, "Thy kingdom come." You have heard it hundreds of times in scripture, prayer, hymn, and sermon. You may even have studied its meaning in church school. But now what does it mean? If you have a few extra minutes, try your hand at writing a paragraph on the precise meaning of "the kingdom," as Christians understand it.

If it were a term lying out on the edge of our Christian faith, we would not have to care so much whether we understood it or not. But it lies very close to the center. The pages of the New Testament are full of it. In the Gospel of Matthew alone it occurs almost fifty times. You will find it in the New Testament in various forms—"the kingdom of heaven" (typical of Matthew), "the kingdom of God" (typical of the other Gospels), and sometimes merely "the kingdom." Jesus talked about it constantly. At the very beginning of Jesus' ministry we read: "From that time Jesus began to preach, saying, Repent, for the kingdom of heaven is at hand" (Matthew 4:17). And on the night before his crucifixion he said to his disciples at the Last Supper, "I shall not drink again of this fruit of the vine until that day when I drink it new with you in my Father's kingdom" (Matthew 26:29).

What do Christians mean by "the kingdom"? And what does it mean to us?

What the Kingdom Means

The best clue to our understanding of "kingdom" is the fact that this English word originally meant both "kingdom" and "kingship." So did the corresponding Greek word, "basileia." In the Revised Standard Version of the New Testament, you will find this word translated in Luke 19:12 as "kingly power," which is much like "kingship." What we are after is closer to this latter meaning, than to the former meaning. When we speak of the kingdom of God, we are not to think of an area running so many miles from this river to that mountain range; nor of a political unit such as the kingdom of Belgium. What we have in mind rather is a state of affairs, in which God's kingship or lordship is acknowledged by people generally and all of life comes under his rule.

"King" is not the best word to use in referring to the Christian God. But he is thought of as a kindly king, a fatherly king. Perhaps if we said "the fatherhood of God," and meant by that a state of affairs in which people gladly recognized God as their Father and lived accordingly, we should not be far off the track. But we had better stick to "kingdom," because that is the word that has been used traditionally, and is still familiar. In proportion as people accept God's gracious rule and give themselves to his will, the kingdom comes. Or, to use different words for the same idea, in proportion as people take this step, they enter into the kingdom.

A very simple definition of the kingdom is to be found in the Lord's Prayer. There we say: "Thy kingdom come, thy will be done, on earth as it is in heaven." Generally we repeat these words all in one breath, for they belong together. The second sentence enlarges upon the first. It tells us what the first sentence means.

The kingdom, then, is both God's concern and our concern. He is the king. It is his kingdom. His will and rule are its law. He thought of it first. We make bold to believe that God dreamed of such a state of affairs, long before the idea ever entered the mind of man. In fact, men got the idea from him, as they tried to trace out his purposes for the world. And God has been working for the kingdom longer and harder than we can ever hope to do, and still continues to work for it. But it is also our concern. We are its members. Among us the kingdom is being built. Only as we accept God's rule, does the kingdom come. Only as we turn to God in childlike trust, do we enter into the kingdom and expand its "borders." Jesus said this clearly in the words, "Whoever does not receive the kingdom of God like a child shall not enter it" (Mark 10:15). We can hasten the coming of the kingdom, or retard it. Apart from us, it does not come.

In a sense the kingdom is here now; and in another sense its realization is in the far distant future. Any person who comes to God in childlike trust and lives accordingly, is in the kingdom. Any group of people, such as an earnest company of believers in a Christian congregation, who accept God's rule for all they do and are, belong to the kingdom. In all such spots the kingdom is already in some measure a reality. But the full realization of this great dream when all men shall live together as brothers under God as their common Father—that seems to be a long way off. Look how we fight one another, cheat one another, mistrust one another! Think of how indifferent we are to one another's sufferings! And how often we ignore God, and his will for our lives! The fullness of the kingdom is still beyond our sight. You and I will never live to see it. A hundred thousand years from now it may still be on the way. Perhaps it will never arrive in its perfection on this earthly scene. But we are to keep on trying, even as God does.

In one sense the kingdom is inside our own persons; and in another sense it is outside us in the ways we arrange and handle our life together. The kingdom starts within us, one by one. It is a matter of how we individually feel toward God and toward one another. But it shows itself unmistakably in the way people live together, the laws they make, the business practices they follow, the customs they accept, the manner in which they settle disputes among nations. Here is a long list of facts concerning the United States during the years just before the mid-point of the twentieth century. How many of these fit the kingdom of heaven? How many are in accord with God's rule? How many of them picture individuals turning toward God as Father and their fellow men as brothers?

In World War II, which had just finished, the United States spent $300,000,000,000. (How would people spend their money in the kingdom of heaven?)

There were 18,400,000 veterans of past wars in the United States. (How many veterans of former wars would there be in the kingdom of heaven?)

America was spending $1,250,000,000 a year on its churches;

$1,565,000,000 a year to see motion pictures;

$3,000,000,000 a year on public schools;

$3,880,000,000 a year on tobacco;

$9,640,000,000 a year for alcoholic drinks (this sum would have fed 25,000,000 starving people for a solid year, giving each one two quarts of milk a day, two loaves of bread, and other necessary food);

$15,000,000,000 a year on various types of gambling;

$15,000,000,000 a year on military appropriations;

$15,000,000,000 a year, or more, to pay the costs of crime and delinquency. (Is all this about right for the kingdom of God?)

There were about 75 anti-Semitic newspapers in the United States.

During World War II, 18.2 per cent of Negro registrants were classified 4F, whereas only 8.5 per cent of white registrants were so classified; in other words, Negroes lived under conditions which left them less fit, physically and mentally, than white people.

50,000,000 comic books were being sold each month (containing such "comical" sights as the blood-stained face of a victim whose eyes had been gouged out).

9,000,000 children were attending the movies each Saturday afternoon. (Were the pictures they saw about what one would expect in the kingdom of heaven?)

The people of the United States were drinking on an average more than twenty gallons of alcoholic beverages each year.

In one of our largest cities, three-fourths of the dwellings for Negroes were sub-standard.

In another large city during World War II some of the draft boards had their offices in downtown hotels. Negroes who came to register to fight for democracy had to use the rear doors and the freight elevators.

4,000,000 children in the United States of school age were not in any school.

In a good post-war year the average wage of a worker in a factory was $1.18 an hour. This seems like a good deal; but for fifty weeks of forty hours each it amounts to only two-thirds of what was needed for a decent life for a family of father, mother, and two children.

The top two-fifths of the people of the United States got 70 per cent of the national income; the bottom two-fifths got only 15 per cent. (Are these about the right proportions for the kingdom of heaven?)

7,000,000 families in our country were getting along on an average annual income of $835.

The number of divorces each year was running a little more than one-fourth the number of marriages.

Remember that the foregoing statements apply only to the United States. In many ways we have been blessed above the other nations of the earth. And in many respects we have worked out a pattern of life which seems to be more just, decent, and brotherly than in some other places; and hence more in keeping with God's will. So we have a long way to go, both in our own nation and in the world, before we are even close to the kingdom of heaven. For the kingdom means that not only individual lives but also the common life of mankind must come under God's rule.

Some Doubtful Notions

During the last half-century, some people have thought of the kingdom as being identical, to all intents and purposes, with a certain political or economic system in which they were deeply interested. The kingdom, some of them said, means principally democracy. Get a democratic form of government, with everyone privileged to vote and all officials responsible to all the people, and the kingdom will be here. But it isn't that easy. Most of us believe that democracy is actually closer to the will of God for his children than totalitarianism. But even in a democracy citizens can stay away from the polls in droves, and officials can look out for themselves and their friends rather than for the common good.

Others have said that the kingdom means principally socialism. Put the ownership of mines, factories, banks, railroads, oil wells, and the like in the hands of all the people instead of a few, and the kingdom will be here. But it isn't quite so simple as all that. Some Christians believe sincerely that socialism is closer to God's purposes than capitalism, while others think just the opposite. But one thing is sure: there is no guarantee that the politicians who run mines under socialism and the laborers who work in them will be any better at heart than mine owners and mine workers under capitalism.

No system, however good, is good enough by itself; it still needs good people to run it. And no system is identical with the kingdom of God. Mere prosperity is not identical with the kingdom of God. If every family in America owned two automobiles, and had chicken every day for dinner, the kingdom would not necessarily be here. The central idea of the kingdom is childlike acceptance by all men of God's fatherly rule.

Some people look for the kingdom to be ushered in dramatically, with Jesus' return in the clouds in glory. This idea has been present in the Church for a long time, in fact, from the very beginning. Before Jesus' day the Jews, who have been under the heel of some conqueror or other most of the time, looked for a Messiah who would put all their enemies to flight and bring in a wondrous new day. In the Early Church the Christians, in the grip of frightful persecutions, kept looking toward the skies for the triumphant return of their Lord. In our own day we still have groups of sincere people who earnestly await Jesus' second coming. They distribute literature and make radio broadcasts, raising questions in the minds of many young people, as well as older ones. Now you can find this idea in the pages of the New Testament. But as the centuries went by and Jesus did not return in visible form, the Church for the most part settled down to another conception, namely, that of the slow coming of Jesus' spirit into individual lives and into our common life. This is probably the better way to view the matter. Notice what Jesus himself said: "Being asked by the Pharisees when the kingdom of God was coming, he answered them, The kingdom of God is not coming with signs to be observed; nor will they say, Lo, here it is! or There! for, behold, the kingdom of God is in the midst of you" (Luke 17:20-21).

Some people at times have thought the kingdom will come about almost automatically. It is bound to come. The process of evolution is a sort of escalator, which is irresistibly headed upwards. Nothing can stop it. Generally speaking, this idea has flourished mostly in times of peace and prosperity, such as those before World War I, or during the good years of the 1920's. But it seems more and more unreal in the distress and uncertainty of our own day. The goose does not hang quite so high nowadays. We are by no means so sure of ourselves. We now know from bitter experience that we have it in our power to give man's hopes and God's plans a terrible setback.

On the contrary, when times are bad, as in the days before, during, and after World War II, the opposite notion gets abroad. Some people have given up all hope of the kingdom's ever coming here on this earth, or even drawing much closer than it is now. This notion was first preached and taught in recent years in Europe, where the best that man could do ended only in defeat and endless misery. From there it spread to America. But this too is going to extremes. There is no point in underestimating God. We can delay his purposes by our own sinfulness, but we can scarcely block them completely. The poet has written words which we do well to remember when days grow dark, and the hope of the kingdom becomes dim:

> Keep heart, O Comrade: God may be delayed
> By evil, but He suffers no defeat;
> Even as a chance rock in an upland brook
> May change a river's course, and yet no rock—
> No, nor the baffling mountains of the world—
> Can hold it from its destiny, the sea.
> God is not foiled; the drift of the World Will
> Is stronger than all wrong. Earth and her years,
> Down joy's bright way, or sorrow's long road,
> Are moving toward the purpose of the Skies.

Seek First the Kingdom

Youth is a time of making major decisions, but the chief one of all is what shall come first. You can't put everything first in your life, any more than you can get in a car and drive rapidly off in all directions. Only one thing can come first. What shall it be? To get ahead in the world? To make money? To have a good time? Or something else?

Jesus' answer is all too plain: "But seek first his kingdom and his righteousness, and all these things shall be yours as well" (Matthew 6:33). He seems to be saying: "Set your heart on the kingdom; give yourself to it with no if's, but's, or and's; and everything else you really need will take care of itself." The kingdom of heaven is the grandest dream ever to enter the mind of man. There is nothing else so fine, or so big, or so worthy of our utmost allegiance.

If you were to seek first the kingdom, what would this mean when you come to choosing a vocation? Are there some vocations which advance the kingdom clearly and unmistakably? Are there others which are neutral, neither helping nor hindering much? Are there still others which actually hold back the realization of the kingdom? Once more, are there vocations which promote or retard the kingdom, depending upon how they are carried out?

If you were to seek first the kingdom, would this fact color in any way your relationship to the Church? How important

94

is the Church to the kingdom of God? Among all the places in the community where you can labor for the kingdom, how does the Church rank? How large a claim, therefore, does it have upon you?

If you were to seek first the kingdom, would this have any effect on your school-work? Can a poorly prepared person render effective service in hastening the day when men shall live together as brothers under one Father? Is there anything in this dream to keep you at your studies faithfully, and help you enjoy them?

If you were to seek first the kingdom, would this have any bearing on the way you spend your spare time? Can you name some leisure-time activities which are in full harmony with the kingdom of heaven? Can you name some that don't fit at all?

If you were to seek first the kingdom, would this shape your attitude toward people of other races? How would people of different races feel toward one another if the kingdom were fully realized? How close is your community now to such a relationship? How close are you?

If you were to seek first the kingdom, would this determine your use of money? From the standpoint of the kingdom of God, what is money for? Whose money is it?

If you were to seek first the kingdom, would this affect the content of your daily prayers? Would you find yourself wondering each morning what you could do this day to advance God's kingdom, and inquiring each night whether you had grown that day in your fitness for the kingdom?

8

*Many are the afflictions of the righteous: but the
Lord delivereth him out of them all.*

—PSALM 34: 19

WHY DO THE RIGHTEOUS SUFFER?

There are parts of a ship which left to themselves would
sink. The engine, the shafts, the steel girders,—all taken
out of the ship would settle to the bottom of the sea. But
when those heavy steel parts are built into the frame of
a ship, the ship floats. So it is with life. That wound of a
friend, that business failure, that son's death,—such sorrows
taken singly would sink us; but when these are fitted into
the framework of life whose builder and maker is God,
they keep afloat. Yes, all things, good and bad, can be carried on the voyage of life, if we keep our love and trust in
the goodness of God.

—RALPH W. SOCKMAN

SEVERAL years ago a check-list of possible subjects for discussion was given to a young people's group. The topic
checked most often was, Why do good people suffer?

Ordinarily we do not bother so much over the suffering of
bad people. We are inclined to say that they had it coming
to them, and let it go at that. But the suffering of good people,
that is harder to account for. We waste little sympathy on the
man who will not work, and goes hungry. But what about his
children, who have done nothing to deserve such a fate? We
merely shrug our shoulders when we read of serious injuries
to a drunken driver in an automobile collision. But what
about the people in the other automobile? We can't quite
shrug that off.

Perhaps we should be more concerned over the lazy man and the drunken man than we are. Why did they turn out as they did? If life had been set up a little more justly, with a little more incentive set before the eyes of the lazy man in his youth, and a little more happiness poured into the life of the drunken man, maybe they would not have become a loafer and a drunk respectively.

Nevertheless, our chief concern is with the ill fortune of the righteous. How can we account for that? How can we reconcile it with the goodness of God? Why does a good God let it happen?

There is no answer to these questions that is altogether satisfactory. Certainly no one answer is enough. We shall examine several. But when we are through we shall have to admit that we don't know all the answers, and for the rest fall back simply on our trust in God.

Somebody Was Sinful

A great deal of the world's suffering is due simply to the fact that somebody sinned. And the person who does the suffering is not always the same as the person who did the sinning.

A denominational filmstrip produced recently tries to dramatize the distress of millions by inserting at several points the picture of one Chinese child, seated alone on the ground with his mouth wide open in a cry of fear and starvation. The accompanying record carries the sound of a baby's anguished wail. The first time you see and hear this little fellow, you may be inclined to titter, out of self-consciousness, perhaps. But not the second or third time! After a while you get to thinking. Why should a helpless, innocent baby like this have to starve to death? If grown people insist on fighting, let them go to it; they at least walk into it with their eyes open. But this baby has done nothing to bring on his own troubles. Why does God allow such a thing to happen?

God doesn't want such a thing to happen, and he didn't

make it happen. Instead he put enough good soil on the earth, and provided enough sunshine and rain to make food for this baby and all the others like him. And he also arranged to have him born into the shelter of a family circle, where the father and mother in normal times would see to it that he got enough to eat. But God also made us free to choose either good or evil. Around 1940 the human race seemed to be working overtime at choosing the evil. The armies of Japan invaded this child's homeland. Some crops were never planted. Others were destroyed, or stolen. Homes were demolished. Families were separated. Untold thousands of people were killed. In due time civil war broke out. Communist armies marched south. Chinese officials sometimes fattened their own purses with supplies that should have gone for relief. Americans gave heavily to ease the suffering, but not heavily enough to hurt themselves or to feed all the hungry. And so a baby sits on the ground in pain and terror. Why? Because we are not as yet good enough to get along with one another or to care for one another.

The first answer, then, to the question of why the righteous and innocent suffer is the old-fashioned, three-letter word, "sin." And because we are all so closely bound together, the consequences of a person's sin cannot always be confined to him. They often reach out and strike others who are innocent.

Someone Was Ignorant

A modern novel takes for its setting the period and events of the Revolutionary War. The leading characters are three young men who became medical doctors. They never saw the inside of a medical school, but merely served an apprenticeship with old established doctors and hung out their shingles. The medical knowledge of the day was quite primitive, judged by our modern standards. There was, for example, no use of anesthetics. If an operation had to be performed, the patient simply had to endure the pain and shock as best he could. One especially pathetic incident involved a little girl, the daughter of a sea captain. While playing one day, she fell down the stairs and broke her forearm in a compound fracture, so that the jagged splinter of bone stuck out of the flesh. In those days the usual treatment in such cases was to cut the arm off. One of these young doctors was called in on the case. He was constantly reaching out for improvements on the crude practices of his day; so he resolved to try to save the arm. Probably he would have succeeded, had he not fallen ill and been unable to attend the little girl for a few days. During his absence an old-line doctor took his place—and cut off the arm. And so a little child had to grow up into girlhood and womanhood crippled and deformed. Why? Because people were not good enough? No; because they were not wise enough.

A considerable portion of human suffering can be laid to this cause. If we only knew more of life's secrets, we could avoid much suffering or relieve it. But our knowledge is incomplete, and the suffering continues. Years ago smallpox was greatly feared. Many people were disfigured by it, and some were killed. Now every child is vaccinated and smallpox is almost unknown. The suffering due to smallpox is slight indeed, because our knowledge is increased. Until quite recently pneumonia was a dread illness, but now penicillin takes hold of most cases of pneumonia in a manner almost miraculous.

Nor is it only bodily suffering which results from ignorance. A leading psychiatrist, who during World War II had many contacts with boys who went to pieces nervously or emotionally, has written a sharp criticism of the mothers of these young men. He holds that they are responsible for their sons' breakdown. They babied their boys too much. They shielded them from life. They tied them fast to their own apron strings. When the hard realities of war came along—or even of training camp—the sons couldn't take it, and suffered immensely. According to the psychiatrist, it was largely the mothers' fault. If he is right, we have another instance of suffering due to ignorance. These mothers were not sinful,

although there may have been some selfishness in their cling-
ing to their sons. They were chiefly ignorant. They did not
know enough about the laws of psychology to do what was
best for their boys. The result was suffering for sons and
parents alike.

Such suffering does not come from God. He has left all
sorts of clues lying around to help us discover the secrets of
life. But it takes us a while to find them. Meanwhile people
suffer.

Good Laws Sometimes Harm

The explanations we have brought forward thus far don't
take care of all possible cases of suffering by any means. Suppose, for example, that a bricklayer is working on a wall some
fifteen feet above the ground. At the foot of the wall his
helper is bending over, getting some more bricks to take up
the ladder. As the bricklayer leans over to put a brick in
place, a sharp gust of wind makes him lurch forward and lose
his hold on the brick. It falls on the helper's head, and kills
him. What, now, was it that cut this young man's life short,
and brought suffering and sorrow to his family? You can
hardly say that it was sin. The bricklayer did nothing selfish
or hateful. He did not wish to hurt his helper, or anyone
else. The helper likewise had done nothing wrong. It is hard
to find any sinful intentions in a case like this, anywhere
around the circle. Nor was it ignorance which caused the suffering. The death of this worker, and the attendant suffering,
were due to the law of gravity, plus a gust of wind at the wrong
time. Now the law of gravity is a very good idea. By and large,
it works out for the well-being of God's children. Without it,
we couldn't build a house, for it would simply float off into
space. We couldn't stand still long enough to hold a con-
versation. There would be no stability to our lives at all. But
in this instance, a generally good law made a brick fall, and
a man was killed.

Suffering of this sort can scarcely be held against God. It is hard to see how any guarantee could be worked out against the best of laws and forces "backfiring" occasionally. Fire keeps us warm, and cooks our food; but it can also burn us terribly. Rain waters the earth, and helps to produce our crops; but it can swell a stream and drown people. The sun is our very life; but it can cause sunburn and sunstroke. Sometimes, of course, our own carelessness enters the picture; but there are other cases where that is not true. Then all we can say is that a good law, which ninety-nine times out of a hundred operates to the benefit of mankind, hurts somebody the hundredth time.

A widowed mother, a very devout church member, had an only son who was an electrician. One day he touched a high-voltage wire, and was instantly killed. In her grief she wondered why God had done this to her. Had she not tried long and hard to be a good Christian? We can sympathize deeply with the mother's sorrow, and also with her bewilderment. But God did not do this to her. He did put electrical energy into the universe, and laid down the laws by which it operates. By and large, electricity is one of our most useful servants. We can be most grateful for it. But any person who touches a high-voltage wire will get shocked, whether he is good or bad. The mother can hardly expect God to prevent this from happening. She can believe that he is with her in her suffering, and that her son is in his safe-keeping.

Trials Make Us Strong

We must now turn back to the beginning, and raise a fundamental question: Would it not have been possible to create a world without so many difficulties and dangers? Any one of us can picture such a world, and the delights of living in it. To begin with, there would be no disease germs, and no viruses. So at one stroke we would eliminate diphtheria, pneumonia, typhoid fever, tuberculosis, and most of the illnesses we now know. Then some ordinary nuisances could well be done away with, such as flies, mosquitoes, and snakes.

We could surely get along very well without them. Earthquakes, tornadoes, hurricanes, and lightning could go also, leaving life much safer and happier. And weeds!—we could dispense with them quite nicely, and the gardener and the farmer would have a far easier time of it. Since we have gone as far as this, we might as well go a little farther and rig up a truly idyllic existence. Why not get rid of these extremes of temperature, which cause us so much discomfort, and make us spend money and effort to keep warm in winter and cool in summer? About seventy degrees Fahrenheit the year around would be satisfactory! And all sickness, even the possibility of sickness—how happy life would be without it! Good health would then be automatic; nobody could miss it. And all sin, even the possibility of sin—let that go too. And all unhappiness, even the possibility of unhappiness! That would round out the list. With no danger and no difficulty, and health, happiness, and goodness guaranteed for all, surely then life would be worth living. Why, we may say, didn't God think of all this himself?

Maybe he did; and maybe he decided against it, because he loves us. There is one thing wrong about such a scheme: about all it would ever produce is jellyfish. Certainly it would never bring forth strong men and women, sons and daughters of God, people with backbones not only in their bodies but also in their souls. Placid, contented, animal-like creatures—yes; perfect, smooth-running machines—yes; but strength of character and personality—no!

During World War II a young soldier lost both his hands in the sudden explosion of a bomb. So courageously has he learned to live with artificial hands, that he took the leading part in a motion picture describing the rehabilitation of disabled veterans, and he now travels about the country making addresses and inspiring all with his spirit. He has paid a terrible price for this spirit—too terrible a price!—but he has something which will last forever, and which would have been unthinkable in the kind of world pictured above.

No matter whether people agreed or disagreed with the policies of the late President Roosevelt, they all without exception admired the heroism with which he triumphed over infantile paralysis. In the dream world described above, there would be no infantile paralysis, and no heroism.

We come then to a noble idea: God set us in a world of danger and difficulty, not because he hated us, or because he couldn't do anything else, but because he loved us. (A good parent, who truly cares for his children, will not shield them from all temptation and hardship; because he knows that would not be good for them.) This was the only way we could grow in character. This was the only way God could have sons and daughters. So he took the chance of a world in which there would be both suffering, and growth of personality. The former is the price we pay for the latter. God too pays a price. Being a Father, he suffers with us eternally.

Some Suffer for Others

One explanation remains to be considered, a principle which takes us close to the heart of the Christian understanding of life. The suffering of good people often works out for the good of others. We call this "vicarious suffering." The word "vicarious" is from the same root as the first part of "vice president." It means "in place of," or "on behalf of" another.

Examples are easy to find, because all life is full of such suffering. A mother and father often worry endlessly about a wayward son or daughter. The knowledge of their worry is sometimes the only thing that will draw the youth back from his waywardness. The sheer mass of suffering following World War II was too awful to contemplate. Sooner or later such suffering will reach the point where people won't be able to stand the thought of it. Then the diplomats and statesmen will renounce war; and the Chinese baby and the millions of other sufferers will have helped to redeem future generations. In the days when the Mongols were sweeping across

Asia they used to cut a steak from the thigh of a living animal. Over the years the cries of abused animals have finally made such an impression that the Society for the Prevention of Cruelty to Animals will now prosecute a man if he works a mule with a sore shoulder. Animals and men are now better off, because beasts suffered on the steppes of Asia centuries ago. Mahatma Gandhi by his own suffering helped his beloved India to independent nationhood. And Christian faith has long held that Jesus suffered on the cross for the redemption of mankind. (We shall come back to this in our next chapter.)

Suffering, then, seems to have a place in God's plan for us. It has a value, not only for the sufferer, but also for others. Through suffering mankind is lifted upward, or "is saved," from lower to higher levels of living. This is one of the explanations why the righteous suffer. It applies with equal truth to our suffering, to Jesus' suffering, and to God's suffering.

In Conclusion

These are some of the answers to our question, Why do the righteous suffer? We do not know them all. In the final analysis, we can only believe that God is good and that some day he will make plain what we do not now understand. A young minister was once called upon to preach a funeral sermon for a mother who died in the prime of life, leaving behind her a husband and three young children. The text he chose was Proverbs 3:5: "Trust in the Lord with all thine heart; and lean not unto thine own understanding." It was a good text. Time and again, when suffering comes, that is about all we can say or do.

We can be sure of one thing, namely, that God does not thoughtlessly or heartlessly inflict pain or misfortune upon us. The God whom we have come to know in Jesus could not possibly do such a thing. Even before our Lord's time people had risen to a higher stage of faith than to believe this of

God. "For he doth not afflict willingly nor grieve the children of men" (Lamentations 3:33). Rather he goes with us all the way, and shares our suffering with us.

It may be that in a hundred or a thousand years from now we shall understand the difficulties of this earthly life a little better than we do at present. There is an old hymn which contains the words, "Some day we'll understand." Perhaps we shall. When we can look back upon these years from a vantage-point beyond them, we may be able to see how everything fits together well, and how even the worst trials have turned out for the good of all concerned. And when we have gone on for a few centuries or so penetrating ever closer to the heart of God's gracious purposes, we may realize that even in our suffering these purposes were working themselves out in ways helpful to us.

Let us go one step further. People have often supposed that in the life to come the injustice and unfairness of this present life will be set right. The good people who suffer here may have a chance at everlasting joys hereafter. And the bad people who seem to have had a pretty enjoyable time in this life may find their badness catching up with them in the life to come. This point of view may contain much truth. After all, if we believe in immortality, the years we spend in this body are just a small part of the whole story. It is the entire story that counts—not just the first chapter. It sometimes happens that a boy or girl is looking forward eagerly to the summer vacation, only to fall ill the day after school closes and spend that entire week in bed. This is a bitter disappointment, and along about Wednesday or Thursday the patient may complain bitterly that life is cruel and he is being cheated at every turn. But then he recovers, and sets out to do all the interesting things he had planned. By the time September rolls around, the vacation months are full of happy memories. It is the entire summer that counts—not just the opening week.

But all this lies in the distant future. Meanwhile, there is much we do not know or understand. And so we fall back in simple trust upon our faith in God. There is one whole book in the Bible which deals with the question of why the righteous suffer, the Book of Job. Here was a good man who underwent almost unbelievable pain and sorrow. His friends came to him with many explanations, but they did not satisfy him. Finally he catches a clearer vision of God than he has ever experienced before. He says: "I have heard of thee by the hearing of the ear: but now mine eye seeth thee" (Job 42:5). Then, and then only, does he find peace of soul. For us also, after we have done our best to explain suffering, there is nothing to do but place our trust in God. He is altogether kind and he is our Father. In his own good time, he will make it clear.

9

Men, what must I do to be saved?
— THE ACTS 16: 30

WHAT MUST I DO TO BE SAVED?

Sinful thoughts and words unloving
Rise against us one by one;
Acts unworthy, deeds unthinking,
Good that we have left undone.

Lord, Thy mercy still entreating,
We with shame our sins would own;
From henceforth, the time redeeming,
May we live to Thee alone.
— MARY ANN SIDEBOTHAM

O love that wilt not let me go,
I rest my weary soul in Thee;
I give Thee back the life I owe,
That in Thine ocean depths its flow
   May richer, fuller be.
— GEORGE MATHESON

IF you were to announce this chapter heading as the topic for a meeting of your youth fellowship, would there be any interest in it? "Why all this talk about salvation?" some might say. "We are getting along all right. So far as we are aware, we have no need to be 'saved.' Salvation is a matter for older people, very pious people, ministers, and perhaps those who are critically ill. The rest of the world doesn't bother about it a great deal. And certainly it's not a major concern to young people."

Nevertheless, this topic cannot be ignored. We hear the

words "Savior" and "salvation" time and again at church. These terms get close to the center of our Christian faith, and deserve the careful attention of old and young alike.

Is Salvation Necessary?

During a single week, newspapers and magazines carried the following true stories of young people:

A very quiet girl of fourteen, a member of a large family, took a job caring for several small children while their father and mother were at work. One of the children, a little boy, began to tease her. He pulled out the electric plug to an appliance with which she was working. Later he pulled it out again. Then he playfully tossed a stick of wood at her. With that, the girl picked up the stick, and beat the boy over the head with it. When he fell to the ground unconscious, she ran in terror to the boy's father to tell him what had happened. The boy died a few hours later of a fractured skull. The girl's mother said she couldn't understand this tragic happening at all, because her daughter was quiet and even-tempered.

A young woman of nineteen developed a "crush" on a major league baseball player. When his team's schedule brought him to her city, she wrote him to come to her hotel room, saying that she had something important to discuss with him. Out of curiosity, he telephoned her, although she was a total stranger to him. She insisted that he come to her room in person. When he arrived, with little warning she produced a rifle and shot him just below the heart. His condition was critical for several days, but he was later reported on the road to recovery. The girl herself seemed not to realize what she had done. Only when she thought he might die, did the meaning of her act come home to her. She seemed clearly to be in need of psychiatric treatment.

A high school boy was interested almost exclusively in sports. As a result, his grades were barely above the passing mark. One day the doctor told him he had a bad heart, and must drop all high school athletics. For a while he found some satisfaction in playing on a team in the town, but his school grades dropped still lower. Then one evening he failed to come home. His parents, after waiting for him a while, went to his room, where they found a note saying that he had left home. For some weeks they heard nothing from him, and did not know where he was. Finally they learned that he had found a job about 150 miles away, and was apparently coming along all right. His high school class just graduated, without him.

These three, and many more, in one week! Obviously they need something. Is it medical care? Psychiatric care? Could it be that they, like us, need salvation?

Have there ever been times when you were deeply unhappy? When life seemed all twisted and confused? When everything went wrong, and nothing went right? When there was nothing to look forward to? When the clouds gathered dark above you, with no silver lining? If so, you need to be saved from something and to something.

Have you ever done things you know are wrong, and done them in spite of yourself? Have you been thoroughly ashamed of yourself, and determined to do better, but found yourself powerless to change? If so, you need to be saved from something and to something.

Or look out upon the tragic mess we have made of our world. Two World Wars in a quarter of a century, and talk of a third. Millions dead, and other millions sick, hungry, homeless, fearful. Large areas of Europe and Asia laid waste. Hatred and tension abroad on every hand. The greatest scientific discovery of all time, the release of atomic energy, not a source of benefit to us, but a nightmare. Our own nation, for all its prosperity, burdened with a tremendous public debt, a shameful crime rate, an alarming divorce rate, and many other symptoms that something is wrong.

There is no doubt—is there?—that mankind needs salvation.

What Is Salvation?

The best starting point for our thinking on this subject is Jesus' parable of the Prodigal Son. You are doubtless familiar with it. But if some of the details have faded from your mind, turn to Luke 15:11-32 and read it through again.

We shall be close to the truth if we say that when the Prodigal Son was in the far country, he was "lost"; and when he was in his father's house again, he was "saved." Now what was he like when he was "lost"? We can set several items down in one-two-three order:

1. His own will was his only law; he did exactly as he pleased.

2. He paid no attention to his father's wishes, and was estranged from his father.

3. He lived quite selfishly, and to a large extent for bodily pleasure.

4. He had a pretty fair time to begin with, but was miserable toward the last.

In any age and in any place, this is what it means to be "lost." This is sin. This is life outside the kingdom of God. This is following the broad way that leads to destruction. As the Bible truly says, many take this way; and all of us stumble onto it more or less at one time or another.

Now what was the Prodigal Son like when he was "saved"? We are getting close here to the heart of our question.

1. His own will was set aside; his pride was humbled (he didn't even ask to be treated as a son any longer, but of course the father wouldn't hear to that).

2. He was responsive to his father's wishes, and was forgiven by his father.

3. He found satisfaction not in his own interests and bodily pleasure, but in companionship with his father and others.

4. He was thoroughly happy.

In any age, and in any place, this is what it means to be

"saved." This is life within the kingdom of God. This is the narrow way which leads to life. It is not so easy to find as the other, but it is worth striving for.

Let us try to pin this down to a definition. Salvation means finding a certain way of life, a certain type of life. The chief marks of this way of life are: deliverance from our own self-will, our self-centeredness, our self-conscious fears and worries; yielding ourselves completely to God's will for us, and knowing his forgiveness for what we have done wrong; finding our greatest joy in a close fellowship with God and a sympathetic fellowship with other people; and a resultant happiness which the ups and downs of life can't touch. In proportion as we find that way of life, and become that type of person, we are saved. In proportion as we miss it, we are lost.

Thought of in this way, salvation is not a once-and-for-all proposition which becomes our possession suddenly and then remains in our possession always without change. Rather it is a growth, a development, a slow achievement. Oh, to be sure, there is a sense in which the Prodigal Son was saved, or began to be saved, at the moment he started back toward his father. In that same sense, we are saved from the moment our lives are headed in the Father's direction. But it may have taken the Prodigal Son months and years to grow fully into the life of his father's house. And so it is with us. St. Paul had been an earnest Christian a long time when he wrote: "I press on toward the goal for the prize of the upward call of God in Christ Jesus" (Philippians 3:14). You see, he was saved; but he was still on the way. So are we saved, if our spirits are headed in the right direction; but ten thousand years from now we shall be more fully saved than we are now.

"But," someone may say, "I thought salvation meant the assurance of going to heaven." So it does! To find this kind of life is heaven, both here and hereafter.

Someone else may say, "Where does Jesus enter into this picture? I thought our salvation came through him." So it does! He has done more to draw us back to the Father's house, and help us find the way, than any other. But that takes us to our next question.

How Does Salvation Come?

Salvation is a joint affair, in which God and man work together. In the parable which we are taking as the starting point for our thought, the son had to do something in order to be saved. And the father also had to do something, or be something. Perhaps what he was had more to do with drawing the son back from the far country than any specific thing he did. Let us consider man's part first, and then God's part.

1. *What we do for our salvation.* The first thing we must do is to repent. But this means far more than being sorry for the things we have done wrong. It means a change of mind, a change of heart, a change of attitude, a change of habit. It means to stop going this way, and to turn around and start going in the opposite direction.

We can see its true significance in the case of the Prodigal Son. We read that "he came to himself," and said, "I will arise and go to my father." Up to this point he had been going steadily away from his father. Now he turned around, and headed back toward his father. That is true repentance.

Or we can see the meaning of repentance in the fascinating story of Zacchaeus, told in Luke 19:1-9. Zacchaeus was a tax collector, who had gotten quite rich by the ancient but not so honorable method of taking what didn't belong to him. One day Jesus came to Zacchaeus' home town of Jericho. Since Zacchaeus was a little man, he climbed up into a sycamore tree, so that he could see Jesus. When Jesus spied him in the tree, he told him to come down quickly. And, much to the consternation of the bystanders, he went home with this sinner. There Zacchaeus said to him: "Behold, Lord, the half of my goods I give to the poor; and if I have defrauded any one of anything, I restore it fourfold." That was true repentance—not merely feeling sorry, but actually changing. Jesus said, "Today salvation has come to this house."

112

Here, then, is the first and most important step to be taken by us. We are the only ones who can decide to take it. And God can't make us take it, any more than the father in the parable could compel his son to turn around and start back home. It is up to us.

Beyond this, the only thing we have to do is to accept gladly what God has done and is doing for our salvation. He is much more interested in our salvation than we are.

2. *What God does for our salvation.* God's part is really two-fold.

In the first place, he shows us the way that leads to life abundant. This he does by a variety of methods. For we are slow to learn, and he must try first along this line and then along that. He shows us the way through the laws of life. If we eat properly and moderately, get enough sleep, and take sufficient exercise, we feel fine; which is God's manner of saying, "This is the right way to go." But if we violate all the laws of health we feel miserable; which is God's manner of saying, "This is not the right way; turn back, and try it again." He shows us the way through conscience. This inner voice can't always be trusted, because it is a part of us and has some of us in it. But deep down it contains a tiny whisper which comes from God, and which we can never quite escape. He shows us the way through the words and the lives of good people. He shows us the way through the Bible, and the Church, and most of all through Jesus, who is the way, the truth, and the life. He leaves no stone unturned to make sure that we find the right way.

In the second place, he shows us his own unfailing love that will not let us go. This probably does more to save us, when we have started to get lost, than anything else. If God were to get angry at us when we go wrong, there wouldn't be much incentive to turn around and return home. But to know that he keeps on caring for us, even when we don't deserve it —that takes hold of us sooner or later.

What do you think it was that made the Prodigal Son de-

113

cide to give up his wild life and return home? Naturally he got sick and tired of living with the hogs; but was that all? Apparently he got to thinking about his father's house, and how pleasant life was there. He was thinking also about his father; at least he composed a little speech to make to him on reaching home. He must have known that he would be welcome at home, or he would not have ventured to return. What he didn't know was that his father was sitting at a window or doorway where he could see the road by which his boy had left, waiting anxiously for him to come back. That picture is Jesus' portrait of God, a Father waiting for wayward children to return, worrying about them in their absence, loving them whether they deserve it or not.

We can see this same force at work between a father and a son today. Suppose the boy manages to do something that provokes his father (it may be teasing a younger sister, or coming home with a poor report card, or any one of a thousand things boys can do). This begins a slight gap of misunderstanding between the two. Suppose now that the father comes down on the boy harshly. This widens the gap, pushes the boy farther away, and increases the chance that he will do something of the same sort again. If and when he does, that widens the gap still more; and so it continues until the two are so far away from each other that neither can reach the other. There is only one thing that will stop that gap from widening and make it narrower again, namely, for the father to begin to treat his boy exactly the way he doesn't deserve to be treated. If he can get across to his son the notion that, while he doesn't like what he has been doing, he still likes him and believes in him, that and that alone will pull him back. A phrase often heard in the Church is "the grace of God." This is what it means—God's continued, unchanging care for us, even when we deserve it least.

How does God make clear to us this love of his that will not let us go? In many ways, some of them quite ordinary; for example, the simple fact that his rain and sunshine come down equally on the good and the bad, those who deserve it and those who don't. But most of all in Jesus! And most clearly of all in the cross! In the crucifixion Jesus carried his own love for people to the bitter end. There he suffered and died for us (it is probably better to say "for us" or "on our behalf" than "in our stead"), and for our salvation. But God was suffering too those six hours, from nine in the morning to three in the afternoon. And so he continues to care for us, and suffer for and with us year in and year out. In Christian faith, the cross opens a little window into the nature of God. So the cross has redemptive power, power to "buy us back" from sin to the abundant life. All of which is well put (as so many things are) in a Bible phrase: "God was in Christ reconciling the world to himself" (II Corinthians 5:19).

Children and young people sometimes get the mistaken notion that God stops loving us when we do wrong; that he cares more for good people than he does for bad people. That is not the way the parable of the Prodigal Son tells the story. God worries more about the boy who goes away than about the boy who stays at home. He is more concerned about the one sheep out in the darkness than about the ninety-nine tucked safely in the fold. There is nothing we can do which will make God stop loving us. And the same is true of whole nations. Any people who seem to us hopelessly wrong at any time are still God's children. They may deny him, laugh in his face, defy his will, but he keeps on caring for them just the same. Day after day he sits at his door, patiently waiting for them to come to themselves and return to the Father's house.

One thing more! The parable says that the moment the father saw his boy in the distance he ran to meet him. The son was doubtless walking, for he was hungry, footsore, and half-sick. But the father ran—two, three, four steps to the boy's one. In a summer conference some years ago the Morning Watch materials carried a verse which refuses to be forgotten:

> Who takes one step toward God in doubtings dim,
> God will advance a mile in blazing light to him.

When we turn our faces and our hearts toward God after any wrongdoing or waywardness on our part, God's love comes out to meet us faster by far than our slow, plodding steps toward him. For a while we may hold out against love like this, but sooner or later we give in and let it draw us back home.

Is a Sudden Experience Necessary?

Sometimes young people wonder whether, in order to be saved, they must have a conversion experience at a particular place and time. The answer seems to be that some people have such an experience, and others do not. St. Paul, for example, certainly did; while Timothy simply had a good mother and a good grandmother and grew up into the Christian way.

Since we all drift away from what is right at one time or another in bigger or smaller matters, we do need from time to time to "turn around," which is what conversion means. But this can happen not once, but a dozen or a hundred times. And it does not have to be accompanied by any particular emotional experience, although it often has much feeling in it.

And since Jesus occupies such a key role in what God does for our salvation, we need to accept him as our Lord and Savior. But this means much more than saying the words. It is a lifetime job. It means repenting as he told us to; following him as best we can; and yielding to God's guidance and love as Jesus makes these known to us. This is the sort of thing that ought to begin when we are little more than babies. It may be sharpened up considerably when we join the church in adolescence, or in some vivid experience of consecration or conversion. But, even so, it needs to go on thereafter as long as we are alive on this earth, and beyond.

Therefore, if any of us have had a definite experience at

a given place or time wherein we felt ourselves to be saved, let us be grateful for it. On the other hand, if we have never had such an experience but are honestly trying to do our part and to accept God's part in our salvation, let us be grateful for that and set our minds at ease. Once there was a young woman who was attractive, popular, and rather favorably disposed toward the Church and religion. But her family and her church expected her to have a special experience, which she just couldn't seem to get. All too early in life, she fell ill and died—still outside the Church. One wishes she might have realized that there are various gates into the city of God, and that the Father welcomes his children through whatever gate they enter.

If we are truly sorry for what we have done wrong, and fully intend to lead a new life, and give ourselves heartily to God's direction and his mercy, we can rest assured that we are safe in God's fatherly keeping.

10

Lord, teach us to pray.
—LUKE 11: 1

TEACH US TO PRAY

Prayer is the soul's sincere desire,
Uttered or unexpressed,
The motion of a hidden fire
That trembles in the breast.

Prayer is the burden of a sigh,
The falling of a tear,
The upward glancing of an eye,
When none but God is near.

Prayer is the simplest form of speech
That infant lips can try,
Prayer, the sublimest strains that reach
The Majesty on high.

O thou by whom we come to God—
The life, the truth, the way—
The path of prayer thyself hast trod,
Lord, teach us how to pray!

—JAMES MONTGOMERY
Scottish hymn writer, 1771-1854.
From Great Companions, *Volume I, compiled by Robert French Leavens,
Beacon Press, Copyright* 1927.

IT is interesting to speculate what would make the deepest impression on a visitor from the planet of Mars to our earth. It might be the Empire State Building, towering above the other mighty skyscrapers of New York City. Or it might be our coal mines and oil wells, assuming that there are no such things on Mars. Or he might be astounded at our airplanes, as they landed and took off from a major airport. Perhaps such an ordinary thing as a field of green grass would impress him most, if he had never seen one before.

But there is a good chance that the most mysterious sight of all would be that of human beings at prayer. We have witnessed it so often that we tend to overlook the wonder of it. What would we think if we were viewing for the first time a person or a group of persons, with their eyes closed, their lips framing words, but the One to whom they were speaking not visible in any direction? To whom are they talking? Where is he? Does he hear? Does he answer? Does their talking do any good?

These and many other questions might enter the mind of our imaginary visitor. As a matter of fact, they often enter our minds also.

What Prayer Is Not

Before we try to work out an understanding of what prayer is, it may be useful to dispose of a couple of false notions.

Prayer is not primarily asking God for something. Some people seem to think that it is. The very question so often heard, "Does God answer prayer?" implies that asking is the chief thing about praying. But that is not the case at all. In order to be sure of this point, all we have to do is to go through the Lord's Prayer, which Jesus gave his disciples as a model for them to follow, and see how much asking it contains. In the Lord's Prayer we begin by speaking to God, and about him. We say that his name is to be held in reverence. We express the great hope of the coming of his kingdom, and the doing of his will on earth as in heaven. Not until we are half-way through do we express any petitions at all, and these are of a most general sort. We ask for our daily bread, which means not merely a loaf of bread but all that we need for our day-to-day existence. We ask that God will forgive us our sins, as we forgive those who sin against us. And we ask that we be not led into any more temptation than we can stand.

That is all! Then our thoughts turn back to God once more, and we acknowledge that the kingdom, and the power, and the glory belong to him forever.

There is nothing here in the way of a request that tomorrow may be a nice day for the Sunday school picnic; or that we may get a job we are hoping for very much; or even that such and such a sick person may be made well. Certain phrases of this sort we would hesitate to insert into the Lord's Prayer. They don't seem to belong to it. The Lord's Prayer is not primarily about us at all; it is chiefly about God.

This is not to say that God is necessarily displeased if we ask him for this or that occasionally. He knows that we are just children, and he may be glad to have us turn to him, even when we have the wrong things in mind and in our speech. A little fellow may run to his father, asking for the moon which hangs bright in the sky. The father does not argue with his boy or become angry at him, even if the request is out of order. The father smiles at him, pats him on the head, and the two are closer together than they were before. Thus it may be with God and us. But our requests to God, beseeching him to do something for us or for the world, are scarcely necessary. He already knows about our needs. And he is already doing all that is possible. If he is a Father, we can scarcely imagine him increasing his efforts upon our request. The main point of prayer does not lie in asking.

Let us go a step further. Prayer is not primarily saying words. It may take the form of words spoken aloud, or words shaped silently by the lips, or meditation that is virtually wordless. When a group of people worship together, they almost have to say words in order to keep together in their approach to God. But in private prayer, the saying of words is strictly secondary. What is primary is the content and direction of a person's thoughts, what they are about and in which way they are heading.

In particular, praying is not necessarily the same as saying prayers. There is a story from the First World War of a soldier who was quite profane in his speech. Finally, things reached such a stage that his chaplain took him to task for his profanity. Now the chaplain must have left the impression of being none too sincere in his own use of God's name, for the soldier replied: "Well, parson, I cuss and you pray, and neither of us means anything by it." The point of this incident is not to justify swearing. The point is that saying prayers and praying are not always the same. We may do the former, and not mean much by it.

Real prayer is a matter of the "bent" of our souls. If what we say we want, and what we actually want, coincide, well and good. But if they are different, it is the latter that really counts.

What Prayer Is

A good definition of prayer is that it consists of a time exposure of the soul to God. Whoever first coined this phrase rendered a splendid service. For these words conjure up a picture in our mind's eye which helps us immeasurably to understand prayer. In a time exposure, the camera is first pointed towards something worth while, and fixed rigidly in that position, and then the shutter is opened and held open as long as may be necessary for the "something" outside to make a lasting impression on the sensitive film inside. That is what prayer is. First a person points his spirit deliberately toward God, and holds it there. Inside is his own sensitive nature, ready to receive an impression. Then he opens the shutter of his mind and heart, and holds it open, until something of God's image is stamped indelibly on his own life. This process may or may not be accompanied by words. But when it is over, his own life is more like God's life than it was to start with. His spirit is more like God's spirit. His will is more like God's will. His thoughts are more like God's thoughts. God has had a chance at him through prayer.

A good example of prayer is Jesus in the Garden of Gethsemane during the agonizing hours just before the soldiers came to lead him away to be crucified. In this crisis he withdrew from his friends, to be alone with God. The words which he said have come down to us, or at least some of them: "My Father, if it be possible, let this cup pass from me; nevertheless, not as I will, but as thou wilt" (Matthew 26:39). Three times he prayed, using these same words. He was opening his soul wide to God. He was facing toward God, so that God's goodness, love, and purpose might register fully within his own life. He was making sure that God's will would be his will in this emergency, and that God's strength would be his strength. In Hofmann's well-known painting of this scene, you can almost see all this happening. Jesus is in a kneeling position, with his hands and arms resting on a rock. His face is pointed upward and outward, for all the world like the face of a camera. Hofmann has portrayed a gentle beam of light streaming down upon him, which may well represent for us the Spirit of God, making its impression upon him. This is prayer, Christian prayer, at its highest.

A good analogy of prayer is Nathaniel Hawthorne's story of the Great Stone Face. You may recall the details of the story. Looking down upon a remote and peaceful valley was the outline of a strong and gentle face, traced out in huge rocks on a mountain-side. A legend, which went back to the times of the Indians, promised that a child would be born in this neighborhood who in his manhood would be the precise image of the Great Stone Face. The central character of the story is a boy named Ernest, who grew into manhood within sight of the Great Stone Face. From his mother he heard the famous legend, and many an hour at twilight he would gaze at the rocky countenance on the mountain-side, and wonder when the human likeness of the Face would appear. Three times in succession, men who had been born in the valley and gone forth to make a name in the world, returned and were hailed widely as the fulfillment of the legend. The first was Mr. Gathergold, a man of great wealth. The next was Old Blood-and-Thunder, a famous general. And the last was Old

Stony Phiz, a successful politician. But each time Ernest looked in vain to find in these men a resemblance to the Face on the mountain. By now Ernest was an old man, widely known for his kindliness and wisdom. He had become unofficial pastor and preacher to the valley, and people came from afar to consult him. It was a poet who had the discernment finally to see that Ernest himself carried the exact resemblance of the Great Stone Face. He had lived in its presence so steadily, that its likeness had been stamped upon him. That is what we mean by prayer.

What, then, shall we do when we come to pray? First of all, think about God. Turn our faces toward him. Turn our thoughts toward him. Turn our lives toward him. At bedtime, we can run over in our minds the many evidences of God's goodness which we have seen that day: sunshine and rain, food and clothing, family and friends, truth and beauty, opportunities for work and play. All of these speak to us of God, and through them we become more aware of him. Our life this day has been lived in his constant care. He has been and is around us and within us, never far removed and yet beyond the farthest star. After we have thought about God for a while, putting our thoughts into words if we care to do so, we naturally turn to our own lives during this day. What have they been like? Have they reflected God's likeness? What sins need to be forgiven? What changes need to be made?

When we pray in the morning, we turn Godward in the same way. This new day speaks to us of God—the brilliance of the sunrise, the songs of birds, the hours of light ahead with all that they will bring us of friendship and usefulness. It is God's day. We see him in it. We think about him. Then our thoughts quite naturally get around to ourselves during this new day. What does he want us to do and be today? What would our lives be like if they resembled him?

Wherever and whenever we pray, this is the basic pattern: opening our souls to God, and giving him a chance at our own lives; thinking first about him and then about ourselves.

123

Prayer of this sort can take place in church, on a hike, in the course of a drive along country lanes or through city streets, during an examination in high school, or washing dishes at home. It may take a half hour, or a split second. If it follows this pattern, it is true prayer.

In the nature of things, we often come to God with some particular problem or burden on our minds. Perhaps it is some moral issue with which we have to wrestle; or some disappointment or tragedy which we have to go through. Jesus came to God this way in the Garden of Gethsemane. But the primary thing is always to lay our souls bare to God. After we have done that, we are in a position to think about our own present need. Then we begin to see the moral problem, or the disappointment, as he sees it. And we begin to get the strength to go through it as he would have us go through it.

We can and should come to God also with other people on our minds. As a matter of fact, we have no business turning to him in self-concern only. God has these other people on his mind. As we become more and more like him, we will too. Have you ever noticed that the first person singular pronoun is nowhere to be found in the Lord's Prayer? There is no "I," "me," "my," "mine." It is always "we," "our," and "us." And so we take with us into God's presence all those for whom we are concerned—parents, friends, the sick, the hungry. We may or may not ask God to do something for them. We really don't need to. It is enough to remind ourselves that he cares for them more than we do, and then to leave them in his safe-keeping. If we have interests of deep concern to us, like world peace, or cleaner dances and athletics at high school, we can take these with us too. We lift them up into the light of God's presence, and see them as he sees them. Then we go out to work away at them, knowing that God is working at them too.

Having done and thought these things, we rest back finally in a sense of peace, like a good swimmer relaxing in the water, knowing that the water will support him if he doesn't struggle too much. We have been face to face with the Eternal. We see our own lives and life about us in a clearer light. We are reminded that around us and beneath us are the everlasting arms. Everything is all right with us, with those we love, and with the things in which we are interested. This is no guarantee against misfortune. It is rather the confidence that, whatever happens, nothing can really harm us. Nor is this the easy peace of dodging hard decisions. Rather it is the contentment of facing them squarely with God's help. And so we rest or work, in quietness and confidence. In his will is our peace.

Does God Hear Prayer?

If a person has an inquiring mind, he may wonder how God can hear so many people talking to him at one time in a hundred different languages. In so far as we think of prayer not so much in terms of the saying of words, but rather in terms of facing our spirits toward him, we have to phrase the question a little differently: Does God know that we are turning toward him? Is he aware of our praying?

Whichever way we put the question, it is not easy to answer. Perhaps we can get a little help from the mystery of radio. If a single radio station can send out messages to a thousand different receiving sets, is it out of the question that a thousand sending stations could register in a single receiving set? There is a poem by Ethel Romig Fuller, called "The Reality of Prayer," which holds out this possibility:

If radio's slim fingers can pluck a melody
From night and toss it over a continent or sea;
If the petaled white notes of a violin
Are blown across a mountain or a city's din;
If songs like crimson roses, are culled from thin, blue air,
Why should mortals wonder if God hears prayer?
—Used by permission of the author.

In the last analysis we must fall back here, as at so many other points, on our faith in God. If there is good ground for believing that God is a Father, then a great many other

125

things follow. If God is a Father, he wants his children to turn toward him. He is happy when they do so, and disappointed when they do not. He is interested in what they say to him, and has doubtless figured out some way or other of hearing a thousand different messages, or a thousand times ten thousand, voiced simultaneously. He is aware of the spirits turned in his direction and enters into fellowship with them.

Did God hear Jesus' words in the Garden of Gethsemane? Was he aware of Jesus' uplifted face and spirit? If he didn't he is something less than a Father; and we are lonely creatures in an overpowering universe.

Does He Answer?

If we no longer think of prayer primarily in terms of asking for something, then this question takes an entirely different turn.

Did God answer Jesus' prayer in the Garden? So far as the first part was concerned, "My Father, if it be possible, let this cup pass from me," the answer was "No." Jesus had to drink the cup down to the bitter dregs. So far as the second part was concerned, "Nevertheless, not as I will, but as thou wilt," God answered it abundantly. Jesus rose to his feet, possessed of knowledge and strength to do and to bear the blessed will of God.

Did the Great Stone Face "answer" Ernest's "prayer"? Yes, in the only way it could be answered, namely, by making Ernest like himself.

A certain professor, in discussing what prayer is like, often made use of a telling illustration. He said that the relationship of a son and his father goes through three successive stages. When the son is a very little fellow, he comes running to his father asking for something he wants. It is "Give me this, father," or "Give me that." The father can't give him everything he wants, but he welcomes his boy and the ties between them grow closer and closer. At a later stage when the son is in his teens, he still comes with requests but they have changed somewhat. He still wants things or the money with which to buy them, but he wants more than these. He asks now for guidance in the perplexities which he faces, and strength to see them through; and he does not go away disappointed. Later still the son is a grown man. He has now entered upon a vocation, perhaps the same as that which his father has followed. Little by little he has grown increasingly like his father, until a real sympathy and understanding binds them together. One day he comes to visit his father. They sit by the fireside, content to be together. The son may not ask for anything at all. The two talk about matters of common concern, or simply sit in silence. The son's main desire is to be near his father, and his desire is granted.

The highest answer we can hope for in our prayers is God himself. If we pray long and hard, if we expose our souls consistently to God, his likeness will be stamped upon our lives more and more. We shall resemble him increasingly. We shall enter into closer and closer fellowship with him. Our lives will become more orderly and purposeful. Bewilderment and anxiety will decrease. We shall live as though we were seeing the Invisible—which indeed we are.

What more can we want than this? This is the Christian life at its fullest. This is the secret of life itself.